Ernst & Young's Financial Planning for Women

Ernst & Young's Financial Planning for Women

A Woman's Guide to Money for All of Life's Major Events

Elda Di Re
Andrea S. Markezin
Sylvia Pozarnsky
Barbara J. Raasch
Freida Kavouras
Paula Boyer Kennedy

EXECUTIVE EDITOR
Jacqueline Hornstein, Ph.D.

John Wiley & Sons, Inc.
New York • Chichester • Weinheim • Brisbane • Singapore • Toronto

Published by John Wiley & Sons, Inc.

Published simultaneously in Canada.

This publication is designed to provide accurate and authoritative information in regard to the subject matter covered. It is sold with the understanding that the publisher is not engaged in rendering professional services. If professional advice or other expert assistance is required, the services of a competent professional person should be sought.

The investment information in this book is provided by Ernst & Young LLP under the oversight of Ernst & Young Investment Advisers LLP, a registered investment adviser with the U.S. Securities and Exchange Commission. A copy of the Ernst & Young Investment Advisers LLP disclosure document (ADV Part II) can be obtained at no cost by sending a written request to Gery Sadzewicz, Ernst & Young LLP, Sears Tower, 233 South Wacker Drive, Chicago, Il 60606.

Library of Congress Cataloging-in-Publication Data:
Ernst & Young's financial planning for women.
     p.   cm.
    Includes index.
    ISBN 0-471-31645-8 (paper : alk. paper)
    1. Women—Finance, Personal.   2. Investments.   3. Widows—Finance,
Personal.   I. Ernst & Young.   II. Title: Ernst and Young's
financial planning for women.   III. Title: Financial planning for women.
HG179.E727   1999   98-47212
332.024'042—dc21

Printed in the United States of America.

10 9 8 7 6 5 4 3 2 1

CONTENTS

ACKNOWLEDGMENTS

The coauthors would like to acknowledge the following people for their dedication and hard work in helping to prepare this guide: Mary Lou Bonney Karp, research and editorial; Debra Englander, editorial assistance; Barbara Hetzer, research and editorial; Francine Abrams, Denis Gaynor, Marc Minker, Colette M. Murphy, Martin Nissenbaum, Charles Ratner, Amy R. Andelsman, Melissa Bertram, Catherine M. Brennan, Deborah DiLeonardi, Patricia Doudna, Molly Jarmusz, Barbara Kane, Robert M. Lia, Lisa Lehman, Celie Macadaeg, Andrea G. Mackiewicz, Helen C. Meehan, Sharon C. Nazarian, Rachel D. Pozensky, Cameron Richmond, Judith Rowland, Laura Rubin, and Gery Sadzewicz.

We wish to thank the leadership of Ernst & Young for believing in the mission of this book:

Philip A. Laskawy, Chairman and C.E.O.

Richard S. Bobrow, Senior Vice Chairman, Assurance & Advisory Business Services & Tax Services

William J. Lipton, Vice Chairman, Tax Services

Beth A. Brooke, National Director, Tax Consulting Services

Deborah J. Kissire, National Director, Tax Sales, Marketing & Special Initiatives

David J. Kautter, National Director, Human Resources Services

Robert J. Garner, National Director, Personal Financial Counseling

We especially want to thank Bill Lipton, whose belief in the concept of this book caused it to take shape and become a reality.

INTRODUCTION

A financial planning guide for women? That's what people asked us nearly every day after we started this project. Are the issues women face really so different from the issues men face?

Well . . . yes . . . and no.

After years of counseling both men and women, we have found that there are numerous financial concerns and challenges faced by women that are unique to our sex. Of course, men face some of these significant issues, too, but often the way they affect women is different from the way they affect men. Consider:

- Women frequently handle the household bills, while men traditionally concern themselves with long-term planning and investing. A surprising number of women don't understand much beyond the rudiments of money management and frequently lack confidence when it comes to making investment decisions.
- Women today are far more likely than their mothers or grandmothers to work outside the home. Still, they earn less than men on average and don't handle their earnings in a goal-oriented way.
- Many women are not planning adequately for retirement—even though women statistically outlive men by 7 years.* In addition, lower pay and time away from the workforce to care for children and elderly parents can mean reduced Social Security and pension benefits for many women.
- More women today are choosing a single lifestyle or life-partner relationships. There are special financial concerns that go with these choices that these women need to understand and act upon.

That's why we wrote this book. *Ernst & Young's Financial Planning for Women* is designed to help women manage their money wisely at all ages and stages. Whether you're single or married, a career woman or a full-time mother, young or mature, your financial future is up to you. And we want to start helping you plan right now.

*Bureau of the Census, projected statistics for 1995.

We at Ernst & Young take the "life-events" approach to financial planning. Depending on your stage of life, you may find certain aspects of financial planning more useful than others. If you've just had a baby, for instance, you may be more concerned about drafting a will and having enough insurance coverage than about many other issues. Similarly, if you're in your 20s, you may feel that a strong focus on retirement and estate planning is premature. The advantage of our approach is that you can pick and choose among the topics. You can focus on what is relevant to you today and then start planning for some issues you expect to deal with in the future. Some of the life events we explore include:

- Getting married
- Dealing with divorce
- Living together
- Widowhood
- Caring for your children and your elderly parents

In the chapters that follow (which we've organized according to the potential events of a woman's life), you'll find practical, easy-to-understand explanations of some important financial planning concepts. What is probate, for example? When do you need a durable power of attorney? You'll find practical steps that will help you implement your own financial plan. You'll read numerous case studies, which we've culled and recast from our collective experience. We hope you'll learn from these composite stories; we believe you will find them compelling. In addition, you'll find a chapter that explains what we term "next steps": how to pick a qualified financial adviser, for example, when you need one. Finally, you'll find a resources section at the back of the book that lists helpful books, Web sites, and groups you can contact.

We don't expect you to read this entire book from cover to cover—at least not right away. Skim through, read, ponder, and study the sections that interest you now. Put the information to use in your own life. Then, when you're ready, come back for more. Our hope is that this book will give you the confidence—and motivation—to take control of your own finances, and that it will serve as a guide to your future financial security.

Ernst & Young's Financial Planning for Women

THE SINGLE LIFE

A re you single? Take this quick test—even if you plan on getting married someday.

Answer "true" or "false" to the following statements:

1. I don't know where my money goes.
2. I've never balanced my checkbook.
3. I plan to start saving money soon.
4. I don't understand stocks and bonds.
5. I expect my boyfriend, live-in partner, or future husband to handle the finances.

If you answered "true" to any of these questions, this chapter was written for you.

In the past, a woman's financial status depended largely on the earning power of either her father or her husband. Her own savings and wages were almost irrelevant—except if they provided her an opportunity to meet a potential suitor. In fact, it was difficult for women to establish their own credit, buy property, sign a lease, or secure a loan without the backing of a male relative.

That's ancient history. Sort of.

Today, women are moving up in the corporate world, operating their own businesses, and running their own lives—without the help of male partners. There are more two-income households than ever before. Still, some women are reluctant to take full responsibility for their own finances. Yes, they pay the bills and their other daily expenses. They even brown-bag lunches so that they can afford that (*fill in your own wish here*) without going into debt. But many women don't think about the long term. When they do, their future plans may revolve around the men in their lives: "I'll worry about supporting myself *if I break up with my boyfriend*", "I'll worry about retirement *after I'm married*", "I'll think about buying a house *when I'm engaged*."

The point is, not everyone meets the right person to marry or live with. You could choose the single lifestyle, or you may not meet that special someone until you're in your 40s. By that point, the lifestyle that both of you are accustomed to will typically require two incomes to support. You've worked hard to build what you have. You probably won't want to take a step backward financially because you fall in love.

No matter what your current or expected future situation is, you are responsible for your own financial future. That future may involve a husband. It may involve children. Or it may not. One thing is for sure, though. That future will definitely involve *you*.

Your E&Y Planner Says:

In my work with numerous clients, I've found that some young women from families in which the fathers primarily took care of the finances (and the mothers managed the family) have minimal experience with money matters. They do not understand the need for managing their own situations. In my experience, the women who do understand the importance of financial independence are generally daughters of women who were widowed or divorced or who worked consistently outside the home. In those cases, however, if the family was adequately provided for by the husband, perhaps through a retirement plan, insurance, or alimony, the daughters often still believe that financial support comes from the man of the house—even if he's absent.

THE INSURANCE ISSUE: WHAT DOES A SINGLE WOMAN NEED?

Every single woman needs insurance. Even if you're healthy and have never missed a day of work. One skid on a dark, slippery road on a rainy night and you could total your car, break both your legs, and be out of work for 3 months. This is a grim picture—but it could be worse. Without adequate medical and disability insurance, you could find yourself in deep debt: debt that could take years to pay off, that could ruin your credit rating, and that could make it impossible to save for your future.

Health Insurance

Like most people, you probably receive your health care coverage through your employer. The kind of coverage you have usually depends on what your employer is offering. Some health care plans are fee-for-service (indemnity) programs. With these types of arrangements, you select your own doctor or health care provider. When you receive medical treatment, you must submit a bill and a form to the insurance company. After you have met your deductible, the insurance company pays a predetermined portion of the bill (usually about 80%) and you pay the remainder. (Your copayment is generally 20% of the total bill.) Often, you'll get an annual out-of-pocket limit that puts a cap on how much you will be required to spend out of your own pocket on medical expenses in 1 year.

Other employers may let you choose between a Health Maintenance Organization (HMO) and a Preferred Provider Organization (PPO). HMOs provide comprehensive service by a single provider, so you have less say about which doctors you'll visit. Essentially you're locked into one group of providers for all your health care needs. But payments are generally lower with HMOs, and you don't have to file insurance claims for each treatment or doctor visit.

A PPO, on the other hand, is a cross between an indemnity plan and an HMO. Under a PPO arrangement, you can pick your own physicians. But you receive discounted fees when you use health care providers with whom the PPO has made special arrangements.

Of course, you could always buy your own coverage, but that's very expensive. Group coverage is generally offered at a much lower cost to you—and is often more complete—than coverage you can buy as an individual. If you're self-employed, you can often purchase a group policy offered through a professional or trade association. Self-employed individuals can get a deduction for an increasing percentage of their premiums on their tax return, thereby having the purchase of their medical insurance subsidized by the government.

If you're young, single, and relatively healthy, think about choosing a higher deductible (if that option is available). You'll pay less in premiums, but you'll still have all the coverage you need.

For those times between jobs, pick up your Consolidated Omnibus Budget Reconciliation Act of 1985 (COBRA) option. It may be a bit costly, but you'll be covered should you become ill before you start your next job. (COBRA coverage, under current laws, continues for 18 months after you leave an employer. Your employer, by law, must explain your rights under COBRA.) In 1998, the cost of continuing PPO medical coverage for yourself through COBRA could be as much as $250 per month. (You need to weigh that cost against the potential for exorbitant expenses should you need unexpected, significant medical care.)

Disability Insurance

Many women (and men) overlook disability insurance. Perhaps they can't imagine being disabled. But the truth is, if you're in your 30s or 40s, you have a much greater chance of being disabled than dying. Unless you have a family who can support you if you can't work for an extended period of time, as a single woman you need disability insurance. You'll be living alone, and you may need to pay for in-home care. Without some insurance to cover your lost income, how will you pay for the rent, groceries, and other necessities?

Many employers have short-term disability plans. Generally, you are considered disabled under these plans if you are unable to perform the regular duties of your job. Coverage can last as long as the plan provides for, sometimes up to 52 weeks. Your employer may also provide long-term disability benefits. If you would like to buy your own policy, or a supplemental policy, you can—but it is quite expensive.

How much disability insurance do you need? You can't buy too much—literally. An insurer won't sell you a policy that covers 100% of your income; otherwise, you might make money by being disabled. Instead, most companies limit coverage to 60% of your gross income. (In Chapter 5, we explain disability insurance in greater detail.)

> **Your E&Y Planner Says:**
>
> If your employer offers a choice of pre- or after-tax payment of premiums for a disability policy, choose the after-tax option. That way, if you are disabled (and not earning a salary), your disability benefits will be tax free. If you're buying your own coverage, any disability benefits paid to you from the policy are automatically tax free. If your employer pays for the policy (or it is paid for with pre-tax dollars), any benefits will be taxable to you and will therefore be less valuable.

You may also be eligible for some compensation from the government. Workers' Compensation, for instance, is a state-mandated program that pays income benefits if you're injured while on the job. Workers' Compensation varies by state. In general, this coverage will pay a maximum of 66.6% of your gross wages or 80% of your take-home pay, up to a specified dollar amount.

You may also be eligible for Social Security disability benefits, but the requirements are stringent. In general, Social Security pays disability benefits only for severe, long-term disability. Most claims are initially rejected. To qualify, you must be unable to perform any substantial work for at least 12 months, or your injury or illness must be expected to result in your death. In addition, there's a 5-month waiting period before you can receive any benefits.

Life Insurance

As a single person, you don't typically need life insurance because you have no dependents. If someone such as your parents or a sibling depends on you for support—or if you have debts—then you must assess your life insurance needs and buy an appropriate policy. (See

Chapter 5 for more information about buying life insurance.) You should, however, consider purchasing a minimal amount of insurance (through your employer or a professional organization) to cover your funeral and estate expenses when you die. Otherwise, someone else will have to pick up that tab. If your employer offers a life insurance policy, this can be an easy alternative. However, in most cases, you can't take this policy with you if you decide to leave the job. A small personal policy may be just what you need. If you have a pet, you'll want to make sure there's extra money in the policy to make sure your pet is cared for.

Long-Term Care Insurance

Long-term care insurance is still rather pricey, unless you can get a policy through your employer. As a single woman, you should investigate this type of coverage, but not until you're in your mid- to late 50s. If you need assistance when you're older, would you prefer home health care instead of a nursing home? If so, make sure your long-term care policy covers care in your home. As a single person, you're used to being independent; you may not want to get stuck having to turn to relatives or friends when you are more vulnerable than you have ever been. So it's good to know you will be able to take care of your own needs. (See Chapter 5 for additional details on how to pick a long-term care policy.)

The Single Woman's Guide to Investing

How much should I save? People ask this question all the time. Unfortunately, there's no easy answer. You need to look at your current lifestyle, as well as your future goals, and come up with a game plan for getting there. If you're single and living in your parents' home, for example, now is a good time to save a large portion of your income since you're probably not yet paying rent, utilities, and some other daily living expenses. Even if you are contributing, your costs are still far below what they will be when you go out on your own.

But how much should you save? You need to do a few calculations. First, draw up a budget of your essential living expenses such as housing, food, clothing, transportation, and so on (see Figure 1.1). How much money is left over from your take-home pay after you've met these

FIGURE 1.1   SAMPLE BUDGET WORKSHEET

Date:_____

To understand where you can cut spending, write down your expenses and label each one as fixed, variable or discretionary. Suggestion: Make copies of this worksheet and update it as your spending habits change.

	Amount	Fixed	Variable	Discretionary
Savings				
401(k), 403(b) or 457 account	$..................	☐	☐	☐
_____	$..................	☐	☐	☐
_____	$..................	☐	☐	☐
_____	$..................	☐	☐	☐
_____	$..................	☐	☐	☐
_____	$..................	☐	☐	☐
Total	$_____			
Housing				
Rent	$..................	☐	☐	☐
Mortgage	$..................	☐	☐	☐
Maintenance fees	$..................	☐	☐	☐
Lawn care	$..................	☐	☐	☐
Repairs	$..................	☐	☐	☐
Home improvements	$..................	☐	☐	☐
Utilities: phone, electric, heat, and hot water	$..................	☐	☐	☐
Property taxes	$..................	☐	☐	☐
Homeowner's insurance	$..................	☐	☐	☐
_____	$..................	☐	☐	☐
_____	$..................	☐	☐	☐
_____	$..................	☐	☐	☐
_____	$..................	☐	☐	☐
_____	$..................	☐	☐	☐
Total	$_____			

continues

FIGURE 1.1 SAMPLE BUDGET WORKSHEET (CONTINUED)

	Amount	Fixed	Variable	Discretionary
Other housing (home furnishings)				
Bedding: sheets, pillows, blankets, etc.	$.......................	☐	☐	☐
Kitchen appliances	$.......................	☐	☐	☐
Cookware	$.......................	☐	☐	☐
Decorating	$.......................	☐	☐	☐
Furniture	$.......................	☐	☐	☐
Electronic equipment	$.......................	☐	☐	☐
_____	$.......................	☐	☐	☐
_____	$.......................	☐	☐	☐
_____	$.......................	☐	☐	☐
_____	$.......................	☐	☐	☐
_____	$.......................	☐	☐	☐
_____	$.......................	☐	☐	☐
Total	$_____			
Food				
Regular grocery shopping	$.......................	☐	☐	☐
Breakfasts, lunches, and dinners bought outside	$.......................	☐	☐	☐
School lunches	$.......................	☐	☐	☐
Coffee, vending machines, snacks	$.......................	☐	☐	☐
_____	$.......................	☐	☐	☐
_____	$.......................	☐	☐	☐
_____	$.......................	☐	☐	☐
_____	$.......................	☐	☐	☐
_____	$.......................	☐	☐	☐
_____	$.......................	☐	☐	☐
Total	$_____			

	Amount	Fixed	Variable	Discretionary
Clothing				
Work clothes	$......................	☐	☐	☐
Casual clothes	$......................	☐	☐	☐
Formal wear	$......................	☐	☐	☐
Accessories: handbags, wallets, belts, scarves, watches, costume jewelry, etc.	$......................	☐	☐	☐
Coats	$......................	☐	☐	☐
Shoes	$......................	☐	☐	☐
Sneakers	$......................	☐	☐	☐
Hosiery/socks	$......................	☐	☐	☐
Underwear/sleepwear	$......................	☐	☐	☐
Dry cleaning	$......................	☐	☐	☐
School uniforms	$......................	☐	☐	☐
Sports clothes	$......................	☐	☐	☐
_____	$......................	☐	☐	☐
_____	$......................	☐	☐	☐
_____	$......................	☐	☐	☐
_____	$......................	☐	☐	☐
Total	$_____			
Insurance				
Life (Person 1)	$......................	☐	☐	☐
Life (Person 2)	$......................	☐	☐	☐
Excess liability	$......................	☐	☐	☐
Long-term care (Person 1)	$......................	☐	☐	☐
Long-term care (Person 2)	$......................	☐	☐	☐
Disability (Person 1)	$......................	☐	☐	☐
Disability (Person 2)	$......................	☐	☐	☐
Total	$_____			

continues

FIGURE 1.1 SAMPLE BUDGET WORKSHEET (CONTINUED)

	Amount	Fixed	Variable	Discretionary
Transportation				
Gas	$.....................	☐	☐	☐
Tolls	$.....................	☐	☐	☐
Vehicle insurance	$.....................	☐	☐	☐
Vehicle insurance	$.....................	☐	☐	☐
Loan or lease payments	$.....................	☐	☐	☐
Car maintenance, washes, etc.	$.....................	☐	☐	☐
Trains/buses	$.....................	☐	☐	☐
_____	$.....................	☐	☐	☐
_____	$.....................	☐	☐	☐
_____	$.....................	☐	☐	☐
_____	$.....................	☐	☐	☐
_____	$.....................	☐	☐	☐
_____	$.....................	☐	☐	☐
Total	$_____			
Medical & Dental				
Insurance	$.....................	☐	☐	☐
Co-payments	$.....................	☐	☐	☐
Amounts not covered by insurance	$.....................	☐	☐	☐
Prescriptions	$.....................	☐	☐	☐
Over-the-counter medicine	$.....................	☐	☐	☐
Vision	$.....................	☐	☐	☐
_____	$.....................	☐	☐	☐
_____	$.....................	☐	☐	☐
_____	$.....................	☐	☐	☐
_____	$.....................	☐	☐	☐
_____	$.....................	☐	☐	☐
_____	$.....................	☐	☐	☐
Total	$_____			

	Amount	Fixed	Variable	Discretionary
Debt				
Education loans	$......................	☐	☐	☐
Home equity loans	$......................	☐	☐	☐
Credit card: credit card balances, late fees, interest, etc.	$......................	☐	☐	☐
Other personal loans	$......................	☐	☐	☐
Mortgage	$......................	☐	☐	☐
Car	$......................	☐	☐	☐
_____	$......................	☐	☐	☐
_____	$......................	☐	☐	☐
_____	$......................	☐	☐	☐
_____	$......................	☐	☐	☐
_____	$......................	☐	☐	☐
Total	$_____			
Children				
Day care	$......................	☐	☐	☐
Tuition payments	$......................	☐	☐	☐
Music and dance lessons	$......................	☐	☐	☐
Little League	$......................	☐	☐	☐
Other after school activities	$......................	☐	☐	☐
Day camp	$......................	☐	☐	☐
Sleep-away camp	$......................	☐	☐	☐
Clothing	$......................	☐	☐	☐
_____	$......................	☐	☐	☐
_____	$......................	☐	☐	☐
_____	$......................	☐	☐	☐
_____	$......................	☐	☐	☐
_____	$......................	☐	☐	☐
Total	$_____			

continues

FIGURE 1.1   SAMPLE BUDGET WORKSHEET (CONTINUED)

	Amount	Fixed	Variable	Discretionary
Entertainment				
Movies, videos	$........................	☐	☐	☐
Theater	$........................	☐	☐	☐
Amusement parks	$........................	☐	☐	☐
Music CDs/cassettes	$........................	☐	☐	☐
Books	$........................	☐	☐	☐
Subscriptions/dues	$........................	☐	☐	☐
Cable T.V.	$........................	☐	☐	☐
Vacations	$........................	☐	☐	☐
_____	$........................	☐	☐	☐
_____	$........................	☐	☐	☐
_____	$........................	☐	☐	☐
_____	$........................	☐	☐	☐
Total	$_____			
Gifts				
Holidays	$........................	☐	☐	☐
Birthdays	$........................	☐	☐	☐
Anniversaries	$........................	☐	☐	☐
Mother's Day/Father's Day	$........................	☐	☐	☐
Valentine's Day	$........................	☐	☐	☐
Weddings	$........................	☐	☐	☐
Bridal showers	$........................	☐	☐	☐
Baby showers	$........................	☐	☐	☐
House warming	$........................	☐	☐	☐
Charities	$........................	☐	☐	☐
_____	$........................	☐	☐	☐
_____	$........................	☐	☐	☐
_____	$........................	☐	☐	☐
_____	$........................	☐	☐	☐
Total	$_____			

	Amount	Fixed	Variable	Discretionary
Personal				
Haircuts	$......................	☐	☐	☐
Special hair styling	$......................	☐	☐	☐
Manicures/pedicures	$......................	☐	☐	☐
Cosmetics	$......................	☐	☐	☐
Contact lens fluid	$......................	☐	☐	☐
Health club	$......................	☐	☐	☐
_____	$......................	☐	☐	☐
_____	$......................	☐	☐	☐
_____	$......................	☐	☐	☐
_____	$......................	☐	☐	☐
_____	$......................	☐	☐	☐
_____	$......................	☐	☐	☐
Total	$_____			
Pets				
Food	$......................	☐	☐	☐
Supplies	$......................	☐	☐	☐
Boarding	$......................	☐	☐	☐
Grooming	$......................	☐	☐	☐
Veterinarian bills	$......................	☐	☐	☐
_____	$......................	☐	☐	☐
_____	$......................	☐	☐	☐
_____	$......................	☐	☐	☐
_____	$......................	☐	☐	☐
_____	$......................	☐	☐	☐
_____	$......................	☐	☐	☐
Total	$_____			

continues

FIGURE 1.1 SAMPLE BUDGET WORKSHEET (CONTINUED)

	Amount	Fixed	Variable	Discretionary
Taxes				
Federal income taxes	$........................	☐	☐	☐
_____	$........................	☐	☐	☐
State taxes	$........................	☐	☐	☐
_____	$........................	☐	☐	☐
Local taxes	$........................	☐	☐	☐
_____	$........................	☐	☐	☐
Social Security taxes	$........................	☐	☐	☐
_____	$........................	☐	☐	☐
_____	$........................	☐	☐	☐
_____	$........................	☐	☐	☐
Total	$_____			
Miscellaneous				
Bank fees	$........................	☐	☐	☐
Annual credit card fees	$........................	☐	☐	☐
Luggage	$........................	☐	☐	☐
Travel	$........................	☐	☐	☐
_____	$........................	☐	☐	☐
_____	$........................	☐	☐	☐
_____	$........................	☐	☐	☐
_____	$........................	☐	☐	☐
_____	$........................	☐	☐	☐
_____	$........................	☐	☐	☐
_____	$........................	☐	☐	☐
Total	$_____			
Combined Totals	$_____			
	Grand Total			

essential expenses? That's the money that *could* be saved. Another approach is to define a percentage or dollar amount of your income that you would ideally like to save, and build your budget around that figure. Most women we have talked to find that this method works better than they think it will. If your budget gets too tight one month or the next, you can save a bit less, but still remain close to your savings goal.

Second, decide on your goal and put a price tag on it. Perhaps you want to buy a home in 5 years. How much will it cost you to do that? You'll need a down payment, for instance, plus money for closing costs. And, if your goal is several years in the future, you need to account for inflation, or rising prices.

Once you know how much money is required, you can go back to your original budget and cut back on your spending if you'd like to reach your goal of buying a home sooner. It's easier to pass up those impulse purchases or another dinner out if you're focused on reaching a defined long-term goal.

As a result of this process, you may find that you cannot save the required amounts, based upon your income and monthly cash flow needs. You must then ask yourself if you are in the right job or the right profession. Are others in your field making comparable salaries? Would a move to a different, but related field earn you a higher salary? Could you perhaps do some freelance work to earn extra cash? Or maybe you need to reset your sights. Make your goals realistic to fit your income.

We all deserve the best, but going into undue debt to get it will only make your lifestyle less comfortable over time. And, if you get married, the last thing you will want to do is bring your old debt into the promise of a new relationship. You'll want to be able to start out fresh. We've seen situations where couples put off their weddings while one partner struggles to get out of debt. Remember that when you marry, the debt becomes the responsibility of both partners. Would you want to marry into a poor credit rating?

Now . . . where should you stash your savings? That depends upon your goal and your time frame. Funds being set aside for retirement, for example, should clearly be put in tax-deferred retirement accounts like 401(k) or 403(b) plans. If your employer matches your savings, you should contribute at least enough to your account to receive the full benefit of any employer matching program. If you do not have an employer-sponsored plan—and even if you do—you should consider an IRA or Roth IRA.

Some women, particularly older ones, feel that safe investments are those where your principal is guaranteed. In fact, women as a group tend to be overly conservative—that is, cautious—in their investing. The problem with this theory is that money market accounts and similar "safe" investments don't historically keep pace with inflation on an after-tax basis. You could be losing principal if the dollar you saved today buys less in the future than it does now.

When choosing investments, you must take into account your risk tolerance level and your desired rate of return. Cash-equivalent investments, such as certificates of deposit (CDs), provide stability and safety for your money—but you'll earn a lower rate of return. Stocks, on the other hand, typically earn a higher rate of return over long time periods. But they also carry greater risk.

In general, the longer your time horizon, the more risk you can take on. You can ride out the ups and downs of the stock market, for instance, if you have more than 7 years until you need the money. But if you need your savings to buy a house in 2 years, you should not take the risk that stocks may go down in value and fail to rebound before you need to cash out. In this situation, you'd do better with a more conservative investment like a 2-year U.S. Treasury bond or certificate of deposit.

In the example in Figure 1.2, you can see the impact that time horizon (the length of time your money is invested) and different rates of return have on a $40,000 portfolio.

The Rule of 72

To figure out how long it will take you to double your investment at different rates of return, use the rule of 72. Here's how it works: Divide 72 by your expected rate of return to determine how long it will take to double your investment. For example, an investment yielding a 4% return will take 18 years to double in value. (Check the math yourself: 72 divided by 4 equals 18.)

When determining your asset allocation, remember the old adage: Don't put all your eggs in one basket. Employer-sponsored plans now offer many investment choices (see Figure 1.3), and, in general, there are literally thousands of choices for your investment dollars. You don't want your financial future riding on the return of just one asset class. Think

FIGURE 1.2 YOUR $40,000* INVESTMENT WILL BE WORTH . . .

	Years Invested	Rate of Return
	5 Years	
$ 53,529		6%
56,102		7%
58,773		8%
	10 Years	
$ 71,634		6%
78,686		7%
85,357		8%
	15 Years	
$ 95,862		6%
110,361		7%
126,887		8%
	20 Years	
$128,285		6%
154,787		7%
186,438		8%

* Lump sum, compounded annually

FIGURE 1.3 FUND TYPE VS. RISK/RETURN

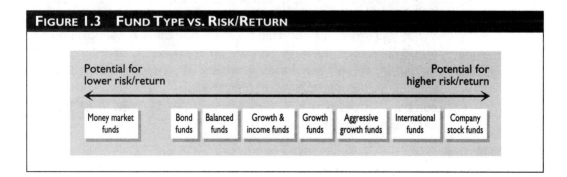

what would happen if the housing market collapsed and all of your retirement dollars were invested in real estate!

A simple asset allocation model is as follows: Short-term savings call for cash (or its near equivalent); medium-term savings call for bonds; long-term savings call for equities. It is also important to diversify. Your equities allocation should encompass different kinds of stocks and/or stock funds, including various large companies, small companies, and even non-U.S. companies.

A Mutual Fund Primer

Mutual funds are a good way to diversify your investments. They provide you with an opportunity to take advantage of a pool of investments managed by a professional manager. So, if you are not an experienced investor or don't have the inclination to become one, having the benefit of a money manager can go a long way for you. You should understand the type of funds you choose and you should be able to follow their performance so that you can make changes as needed. You need to be educated, but you do not need to be a stock market expert. Companies that offer mutual funds receive money from a large number of investors, pool the money, and use it to buy securities. As an investor in a mutual fund, you will own units of the fund, depending upon how much money you have put into it. The units represent an investment in a variety of stocks and bonds, such as the following:

Bond funds invest almost exclusively in bonds. Different funds may concentrate on short-, intermediate-, or long-term bonds as well as tax-exempt, government, or corporate bonds. Please note, however, that bond funds do not have a maturity date like individual bonds do. When you invest in a bond fund there is no definitive sum paid on a particular date as there is when you purchase bonds directly.

Index funds mirror the performance of a certain market index such as the Standard & Poor's (S&P) 500, which tracks 500 large company stocks that are traded mostly on the New York Stock Exchange, or the Russell 2000, which tracks 2,000 smaller company stocks.

Sector funds invest in stocks in a single industry such as technology or health care. This category is typically less diverse than other types of funds.

Growth funds invest in stock and aim for long-term growth (capital gains) instead of current income or dividends.

Aggressive growth funds invest in stock and seek high capital appreciation. These funds do not provide significant interest income or dividends, and are characterized by high risk and a potentially high growth.

Growth and income funds invest in stock and try to balance long-term growth and current income. These funds are also referred to as total return or equity-income funds.

Balanced funds invest in stocks and bonds. These funds have three primary objectives: (1) Conserve principal. (2) Pay high current income through dividends and interest. (3) Promote long-term growth of principal and income.

Other funds hold other types of investments, such as real estate investment trusts (REITs) and gold. If you don't already own real estate, and you feel that it should be part of your investment portfolio, a REIT may be an investment to consider.

Use Figure 1.3 on page 17 as a general guide to help you understand the risk associated with different types of mutual funds. The actual risk and return of any mutual fund, however, will vary depending on the particular fund within any given category.

Another way of looking at funds is through what financial planners call style-based fund analysis. This view divides funds into value funds, growth funds, and core (or blend) funds. Value funds invest in stocks with low price-to-earnings ratios. This means the price of the stock is low compared to the stock's earnings per share. Growth funds invest in stocks with a history of increasing earnings and growth. Although these funds are less stable than value funds, they have more potential for growing your money during a time of economic uncertainty. Core (or blend) funds are a mix of value and growth funds. Many financial planners recommend that you own both growth and value funds to diversify and lower your overall risk.

No matter what savings vehicle you choose, you must pay yourself first to ensure that you carry out your savings program. Most people—even those with the best intentions—are not disciplined savers. Thus, it is often best to establish an automatic savings plan in which money is taken directly from your paycheck or checking account. You can set these plans up with your bank or a mutual fund company. And, of course, your savings plan at work makes this easy through automatic payroll deductions.

> ## MYTH   I'm Too Young to Worry about Retirement Savings
>
> It's never too early to start saving for retirement. By starting early, you can actually save less but still potentially wind up with a larger retirement nest egg because of the magic of compounding over a long period of time. Historically, women have been in the workforce for fewer years than men because they take time off to bear and raise children. It's even more imperative, therefore, that when you are single and working you save as much as possible. Should you get married or settle down with a life partner, substantial retirement savings may mean that you can retire at an earlier age. At the very least, your golden years will be more comfortable. Keep in mind: If you marry later in life, your retirement years may represent the bulk of your life together. You will want those years to be as secure and enjoyable as possible.

ESTABLISHING AND USING CREDIT WISELY

Credit can open important doors for you—or create a lifelong hassle. Just try renting a car or guaranteeing a hotel reservation without a credit or charge card, and you'll quickly get the picture. When you want to buy your first home, you will find that a good, established credit history is essential.

What is credit? Basically, credit is the willingness of a retailer or a financial institution to lend you money. A credit history is the record of how well you have handled your financial obligations over a period of time. Do you pay your debts promptly? To whom do you currently owe money—and how much? Your financial well-being can rise—and fall—depending upon how responsibly you handle credit.

Whenever you apply for credit, the retailer or financial institution will request your credit history. Gathering this information themselves would be too expensive and time consuming, so most lenders rely on credit reports furnished by one of the three major credit bureaus: Experian (formerly TRW), Equifax, and Trans Union.

These reports reveal data about every aspect of your borrowing life—as well as your employment history and any court records related to bankruptcies or tax liens. Federal law requires credit bureaus to erase most adverse information after 7 years. One major exception: a Chapter 7 bankruptcy, which can remain on file for 10 years.

Your Credit Report

Any consumer can get a copy of his or her credit report by contacting one of the bureaus listed below:

- Experian, P.O. Box 2104, Allen, TX 75013-2104, 888-EXPERIAN (397-3742)
- Equifax, Information Service Center, P.O. Box 105873, Atlanta, GA 30348, 800-685-1111
- Trans Union Corporation, P.O. Box 390, Springfield, PA 19064-0390, 800-888-4213

Residents of Maryland, Vermont, Massachusetts, Colorado, Georgia, and New Jersey can get one free copy of their credit report each year—as can all consumers who've been denied credit within the past 60 days. Otherwise, the bureaus charge about $8 per copy in most cases. You can contact these credit bureaus directly. You do not need the help of any other agency or advisor.

As a woman, it's essential that you establish—and maintain—your own credit history. Even if you plan to marry in the near future or if your parents pay most of your bills now, you should have at least one credit or charge card in your own name. Having your own line of credit is particularly important if you become widowed or divorced.

To establish a good credit history, be sure to pay any outstanding loans *on time*. You might also consider taking out a personal loan from the bank. Keep the amount small enough so that you know you can readily pay it back on time. This will prove to future creditors that you can handle debt responsibly.

> ### Your E&Y Planner Says:
>
> Credit clinics (also known as credit repair organizations) promise a quick fix if you've been turned down because of bad credit. These organizations claim they can remove negative information like late or missed payments from your credit report—but they cannot. Here's how the scam works: A credit clinic floods the credit bureaus with requests for information about your file. If the credit bureaus can't respond to all these requests within a certain time, the black marks are supposedly erased. The clinics fail to tell you, however, that the credit bureau can later verify that information (when it has more time) and put those black marks right back on your credit report. So you will wind up with the same bad credit report—plus you'll be out the $50 to $2,000 fee that a clinic generally charges.

Many credit card companies solicit college students on campus, so it's not that difficult to secure that first bank credit card. If you don't qualify for such a card, however, check out your local retailer. Most department stores issue credit cards to shoppers. You'll find that their requirements are generally less stringent than those of a bank credit card issuer.

Once you have a credit card in hand, make small purchases with it and pay the balance off each month, especially if the charges are for essentials like groceries, clothing, and gasoline. (If you consistently pay your bill on time, an added bonus is that it should be fairly easy to raise your credit limit.) You should never pay interest on items that are quickly consumed and that provide nothing of a lasting, tangible value. Once your credit is established, use your credit card mainly for larger, out-of-the ordinary purchases such as furniture, airline tickets, or a winter coat. Use cash to meet your everyday bills, such as food, utilities, or a Friday night at the movies.

If you are paying your balance in full each month, then pick a credit card that charges no annual fee and offers some perk: cash back (calculated as a percentage of the amount charged), frequent flier mileage, or some other award based on usage. Some auto manufacturers, for instance, let you earn points toward buying a car or truck if you use their MasterCard or Visa. Similarly, some airlines let you earn frequent flier miles if you use their cards. Basically, the more you use these "rebate" cards, the more discounts on merchandise and service or other freebies you earn. Or, you can choose a card that makes a small donation to your favorite charity every time you use the card to make a purchase. Call your charity to ask if it offers such a card.

If you pay your entire balance within the grace period, you do not need to worry about the annual interest rate because you won't incur any interest. However, if you plan on carrying your balance over several months for a major purchase for which you haven't been able to save (your television or computer breaks down, for instance), you should comparison shop for the card with the lowest interest rate.

Carrying a balance on your credit card may be necessary for certain purchases or if you're waiting for a windfall payment, such as a bonus, to arrive. But making only the minimum payments *every month* on your credit cards is very costly. Until you pay your bill in full, each month's purchases are subject to finance charges from the date of purchase—not from the date of the bill. When you pay less than the total amount, the usual interest-free grace period no longer applies. (Unfortunately, those interest charges are not tax deductible any longer, either.) Within a few months you will be paying interest on interest. For example: If you were to pay just $100 per month on a $5,000 credit card debt (with an 18% interest rate), it would take 8 years to pay off your bill (see Figure 1.4). Small wonder it seems like you're in debt forever . . . you are!

Credit cards are convenient and, in certain situations, necessary. They can be an excellent way to pay your bills and build your credit rating because they're simple to use and offer an organized and detailed way to

FIGURE 1.4 THE COST OF CREDIT CARD DEBT

The chart shows how much interest you would pay on a $5,000 credit card balance based on 7%, 12%, and 18% interest rates.

Total Balance on Credit Card: $5,000

Interest Rate	Monthly Payment	Interest Paid	Total Cost	Paid Off In
7%	$100	$ 929	$5,929	5 years
12%	$100	$1,966	$6,966	6 years
18%	$100	$4,311	$9,311	8 years

keep your records. You can also gain a small cash flow advantage by leaving money earmarked for your next purchase in the bank, earning interest until the bill comes in 3 to 4 weeks after the purchase is made. But credit cards can severely threaten your financial health if you use them indiscriminately and don't pay off your accumulated charges each month.

Switch to a Debit Card

If credit cards "help" you overspend, try a debit card instead. A debit card works much like an ATM card. (Your ATM card is, in fact, a debit card.) Each purchase, or *debit*, is deducted directly from your checking or savings account, and, in some cases, your brokerage account. The money for your purchase is paid directly to the merchant. It's basically the electronic equivalent of writing a check. (Credit card purchases, on the other hand, are charged. You pay for them at a later date.)

While a debit card can't stop you from spending, it can prevent you from spending money that isn't in your account. Each bank calls its debit card something different—Check Card, Cash Card, Convenience Card—but the cards all work similarly. If your bank doesn't offer debit card services, you may need to switch banks to get a card.

MYTH   All Credit Cards Are Created Equal

Although the terms are often used interchangeably, credit cards differ from charge cards. Charge cards, such as the American Express card and Diners Club card, must be paid in full upon receipt of the bill. (These cards are also called travel and entertainment cards.) No interest is due, but consumers generally pay an annual fee for use of the charge card. Credit cards such as Visa and MasterCard, which are issued by banks, credit unions, and other lenders, require a set minimum payment each month. The remainder of your balance is rolled over to the following month. You're charged interest on that unpaid amount.

Put Your Credit Cards Away If . . .

- You always make just the minimum payment—and, in addition, your payment is often late.
- You don't know how much you owe until the bill arrives.
- You're nearing or already over your credit limit.
- You use the cash from one card to pay off the balance of another.
- You're getting calls from creditors requesting payment.
- You want to make a major purchase, such as a home, and will need a clean credit rating to do so.
- You're using credit to pay for essentials like food or rent.

INVEST IN EDUCATION OR MORE JOB TRAINING

There are two things you can get out of a job: wages and an education. Some lower-paying jobs are worth holding onto, for instance, if you learn new skills. But a job that doesn't pay well *and* doesn't teach you anything new is a dead-end job. That's dangerous for anyone, but especially for a single woman who must support herself.

If you find yourself in that situation, think about retraining. (Your current employer may offer in-house training for a position that interests you.) Or consider going back to school. Relocate, if that school in the city is really *the* place to study. As a single woman, you may have the opportunity to move in pursuit of a career. The more you invest in job training—on the job or through formal education—the greater the chance that you'll be self-sufficient throughout your life. (That's sound advice for women who plan on being single as well as for those who anticipate getting married. Personal and professional growth will help you financially and emotionally.)

Your ability to earn a living will determine some of the decisions you make during your life. If you can support yourself, you will not feel the need to get married so that a man will take care of you: You will be able to take care of yourself. Likewise, if you earn enough to pay the bills and support yourself, you won't need to remain in an unhappy marriage for financial reasons. Money is the means to becoming (and remaining) personally independent.

A Case Study: Making It All Work:
How Penny Paid the Piper

Penny was young, single—and in debt. She was working as a temporary secretary but dreamed of becoming a dancer. She spent every spare moment (and spare dime) in dance class and at auditions.

As you can see from the "before" column in the following budget, Penny's expenses far exceeded her income. Up until this point, her parents had been helping her financially. But they were getting ready to retire and could not help out any longer. Penny needed to make some drastic changes.

When she came to my office for advice, we began the typical financial planning process. We talked about her goals, and looked at her income and net worth. Penny's goal was simple: She wanted to dance professionally. To support herself while waiting for her big break, she worked as a temporary secretary. Her salary was $25,000 per year, which wasn't bad for a starving artist. Still, she just couldn't keep her expenses in line with her income.

Penny thought her biggest problem was her rent. ("It takes such a big bite out of my income," she complained.) I asked her to keep track of her expenses for a month.

A month later, this is what we discovered: High rent was not the culprit. Rather, Penny was overspending in nearly every category. Her phone calls totaled $400 per month; food, $500 per month; transportation, $400 per month; and clothing, $300 per month. We reviewed each category, discussing how much she spent and ways that she could cut back.

We devised some smart solutions. Penny had a large, far-flung family. She called them frequently and talked for hours. Would she consider writing to them instead? Penny liked my suggestion of a round-robin letter. She would send the first letter to her younger sister, who could then add to it and send it to their older brother, who could then add to it and send it to their cousin, and so on. Eventually, the letter would return to Penny, at which point she would take out her first letter and put a new one in.

Six months later, a much happier Penny came back to see me again. She'd applied the same discipline to her budget that she had to her dancing. The result: Instead of running a net deficit, she was now saving more than 15% of her take-home pay.

How had she done it? "I realized," she said, "that my spending had imprisoned me. I thought about how I would feel 20 years from now if I'd had to give up my chance to become a dancer because I couldn't control my spending. I knew I had to give it a shot."

Penny's Budget

	Before	After
EXPENSES		
Rent	$1,000	$700
Utilities	$500	$75
Dance Class	$200	$200
Groceries	$100	$200
Meals Out	$400	$100
Medical	$200	$50
Transportation	$400	$100
Clothing	$300	$100
Beauty	$100	$50
Reading Material	$200	$20
Gifts	$100	$25
Miscellaneous	$50	$50
Total Expenses	$3,550	$1,670
TAKE-HOME PAY	$2,000	$2,000
SAVINGS	($1,550)	$330

BUY A HOME OF YOUR OWN

Owning a home is the last great hurdle for many single women. You may have a wonderful career and a solid investment plan, but do you own a home? Perhaps it's simply that you've waited to find the right person to settle down with. So you've put off the home-buying decision.

But single women can—and should—consider buying their own home if it is something they would really like to do and they plan to keep the property long-term. (Closing costs on the purchase and sale of a home may outweigh the benefits if you hold the home for only a short period.) Home ownership offers certain tax breaks, and has a good track record as an investment: Historically, home prices have increased faster than inflation. Buying a home can be a good investment—and it also provides you with a nice place to live.

Your first consideration should be the kind of home you would like to buy—and can afford. Your three basic choices are a house or town-house, a condo, or a cooperative.

A house is the most traditional property to purchase. Generally, it gives you the most privacy and space. But you're responsible for its upkeep, including renovations and routine maintenance and repairs. For a home that is maintenance free, offers amenities such as a swimming pool and sports facilities, and usually costs less than a house in the same neighborhood, consider a condominium (condo) or a cooperative apartment (co-op).

With a condo, you actually own the unit that you live in. However, you share common areas such as the lobby, the elevators, and the front lawn with the other owners. You pay your own real estate taxes and common charges to a managing agent or homeowners' association. On your annual tax return, you can deduct your real estate taxes and the interest portion of your mortgage, just like you can with a traditional home. You can rent or sell your unit as you see fit.

Co-ops are a bit different. Under this arrangement, you don't own an individual unit. Instead, you hold shares in the corporation that owns the development, which entitles you to "use" a specific apartment. You must pay a monthly maintenance fee to the cooperative corporation, which then takes care of mowing the lawns, paying the real estate taxes, and so on. You are able to deduct the percentage of your maintenance that represents taxes and interest, though, on your annual tax return.

Co-ops have boards, which can—and often do—restrict the way you can use your shares. If you want to sell your shares, for instance, potential buyers are usually subjected to a rigorous financial review by the board. Likewise, the board may limit your ability (as the owner) to sublease your apartment. Because of these restrictions, co-ops are often less expensive than condos. However, the required down payment is often 50% or more of the purchase price.

Getting the Down Payment

As a single woman, you might find that you can easily afford the monthly maintenance of a home (including the mortgage payments and upkeep of the property). But you just can't seem to stockpile that initial down payment. Consider applying for a mortgage insured by the Federal Housing Administration (FHA) (www.hud.gov/core.html). The minimum down payment required by the FHA is less than 5%. (To qualify, the mortgage amount must fall below specified limits.) For more information, visit a local Housing and Urban Development (HUD) office or call the Housing Counseling Clearinghouse at 800-217-6970.

Depending on your family situation, you may be able to borrow some of the needed funds from a relative. Many first-time home buyers receive at least some financial assistance from relatives or friends.

Your family may simply gift you the money. A signed letter must be given to the mortgage lender, however, stating that this gift does not have to be repaid. Or, your family may grant you a loan (just as a bank or another financial institution would). The Internal Revenue Service requires that a minimum amount of interest be charged on loans greater than $10,000, depending upon the financial status of the borrower. You can still deduct the interest—no matter how small the amount—on your annual tax return if the loan is secured by your home. The FHA also permits borrowing from a family member, but such a loan may be subject to certain repayment restrictions and may be recorded as a second mortgage.

You may also use your parents' bank account balance (if they are willing, of course) to help you get a mortgage. Certain banks and brokerage houses allow these balances to serve as collateral for the down payment. If you, the buyer, have adequate income to qualify for the mortgage—but just don't have the money for the down payment—you can obtain up to 100% financing. Your parents must leave their account with the lender until you've paid a certain amount back or there is enough equity in the home to cover a specified percentage of the amount borrowed.

> ➤ **Your E&Y Planner Says:**
>
> If you can't come up with a 20% down payment, many lenders will allow 10% down but require that you buy *private mortgage insurance* (PMI). This can be quite costly. You don't need this insurance once the mortgage falls below 80% of the home's value. Most mortgage holders, however, don't automatically drop the insurance once you have 20% equity built up in your home. You have to arrange with them to terminate the PMI. This may entail an appraisal of your property.

Another option would be to borrow money from your 401(k) plan. Although it's generally not a good idea to sacrifice your retirement savings to buy a house, this type of loan can be very attractive if you don't have any other options. (Keep in mind that the interest you pay is not tax deductible.) Since you're essentially borrowing your own money, you pay the interest back to yourself. A loan won't stop your retirement nest egg from growing—unless you don't repay the loan. Your growth on the borrowed funds is limited to the amount of interest that you're paying yourself, however, so you may miss out on a run-up in the stock market that you could have benefited from had you invested that money in equities instead. Generally, you can borrow up to 50% of your 401(k) account assets up to $50,000, and, depending upon your plan, can take up to 30 years to repay the funds. If you don't pay the money back (which is required if you change jobs), however, you'll have to pay income taxes— plus a possible 10% early withdrawal penalty if you are under age 59½— on the funds not paid back.

If your job provides a significant bonus, which may be larger than your expected salary increases, invest these bonuses over several years instead of using them to buy things right away. This could help get you partway to your goal. If you invest your annual bonus each year (you have $2,000 available, let's say, after tax) and earn 10% annually on that investment, you will have $13,431.22 in 5 years (see Figure 1.5).

FIGURE 1.5 SMALL SAVINGS ADD UP		
ASSUMPTIONS: ANNUAL SAVINGS—$2,000		
ANNUAL RATE OF RETURN—10%		
Year		**Amount**
1	($2,000 @ 10%)	$2,200
2	($2,200 + $2,000 @ 10%)	$4,620
3	($4,620 + $2,000 @ 10%)	$7,282
4	($7,282 + $2,000 @ 10%)	$10,210
5	($10,210 + $2,000 @ 10%)	$13,431

As a single woman you may want to consider a final possibility: a roommate. If you can afford it, it is probably best to buy the home yourself and simply charge your roommate rent. (You could also buy a home that has a rental unit set up.) That additional cash flow will help offset your current mortgage, tax, and insurance costs, but it will bypass the problem of joint ownership if you and your roommate decide to part company. This arrangement also lets you buy a place you can grow into. Many married couples similarly stretch themselves economically in the early years of home ownership because they want to avoid the hassle, and expense, of trading up to a larger house in a few years. This same strategy works for a single woman if she's on a career path in which she expects her income to increase at a decent pace over time.

BEING A SINGLE PARENT

The financial concerns of single parents are similar to those affecting two-parent families: saving for retirement and your child's college education; having adequate life, medical, and disability insurance; maintaining a realistic budget; and executing a will that includes guardianship provisions and, possibly, a trust. (We suggest, therefore, that you read through Chapters 3 and 5 to see what applies to your particular situation.)

You probably have similar costs, too. The difference is that you are the sole breadwinner. Your family's well-being rests entirely on your shoulders.

Because you do not have a partner, you may spend more money on day care or after-school care. If your child is sick, you'll always have to be the one to take a sick day or vacation day. Likewise, if you must work overtime or attend an after-hours meeting, you can't simply ask your spouse to cover for you. You'll have to pay for extended care.

As a single parent, you will probably have a hectic schedule. Working, maintaining a home, and raising a child will fill more than the 24 hours of every day. But as busy as life seems, you shouldn't sacrifice your own goals and needs completely. Even if money is tight, you may need to pay for additional child care so you can go out and relax occasionally—without the kids. (Be sure to take advantage of the child care credit on your tax return or your employer's dependent care plan if you are paying for child care so that you can go to work or attend school.) You may need to spend more on paid services, too, such as an in-home cleaning service and a yard maintenance service, so that you can spend your free time with the children.

One of the most important financial planning issues for a single parent is insurance. You need adequate life, health, and disability insurance because you have a child who depends upon you. Insurance offers single parents protection in case they should become ill or disabled or die.

To cover your short-term cash needs, you could increase your income by temporarily reducing your contribution to your retirement plan. If you fund your own IRA, Keogh, or SEP-type plan, you can defer the decision on how much you'll contribute until April 15 of the next year. Even if you contribute to a 401(k) or 403(b) plan, some plans allow you to reduce your periodic payroll contribution and make a lump-sum contribution before the end of the year. This could be a good use of an annual bonus. (Of course, you need to consider the effect of reduced retirement plan contributions on your ability to retire comfortably when you want to.)

The last resort for increasing income should be borrowing, and this should be done for short-term cash needs only. You can borrow from the cash value of your life insurance policy or your retirement account. You can also borrow against the equity in your home. (The advantage to this type of borrowing is that the interest paid on home equity loans is generally tax deductible up to $100,000 if the loan is secured by the home.)

FIGURE 1.6   SMART RECORD-KEEPING TIPS

One of the best ways to keep your financial affairs in order is to implement an appropriate filing system. That way you have your records close at hand when you need them.

- *Set up permanent files.* These files should contain permanent documents such as insurance policies, rental agreements, and other legal documents that won't change from one year to the next.
- *Set up annual files.* These files should contain documents that pertain to your annual income and expenses such as utilities, medical bills, credit card bills, tax returns, and investment statements.
- *Clearly label your files.* Use a color-coding system if that appeals to you. Some headings that you should consider for your filing system include:

  Canceled checks and bank statements
  Credit card statements
  Utility bills
  Medical bills and reimbursement
  Pay stubs
  Tax returns
  Home improvements
  Investment account statements
  Savings account statements
  401(k) statements and other statements related to employee benefits
  Tax-related material such as charitable contributions, mortgage interest, and real estate taxes
  Insurance policies
  Wills, powers of attorney, living wills, and other legal documents. (These should be copies. The original documents are best stored with your attorney.)

- *Use a safe deposit box to store the following:*

  Stock certificates (if they're not kept with a broker or an investment firm)
  Coins, stamps, and other collectibles
  Auto titles, mortgages, and deeds
  Videotapes or photographs of contents of your home for insurance purposes

continues

FIGURE 1.6   SMART RECORD-KEEPING TIPS (CONTINUED)

- *Don't keep everything.* You needn't keep documentation forever. How long should you hold onto certain information?

    3 years: household bills; credit card statements; receipts for minor purchases

    7 years: canceled checks; check registers; bank statements; pay stubs; tax returns and supporting documentation

    Forever, or until asset is sold: receipts for home improvements, major purchases, and investments; Gift Tax returns; inheritance papers; insurance policies; annual mutual fund statements

---

Being a single parent may mean calling on nonfinancial means of support, such as asking family and friends to help out with child care or home maintenance. This creates another form of debt that you will need to be prepared to pay back at some future date when you have more time or income.

LOOKING AHEAD:
What You Should Be Doing Right Now

No matter what your age, you should:

1. Balance your checkbook and figure out your monthly expenses.
2. Keep track of your important financial documents (see Figure 1.6 for some practical help).
3. Read the money section of your newspaper. Flip through the stock tables.
4. To start saving, pay yourself first when you get your paycheck, even if it's just a few dollars initially. This savings will grow more than you expect.
5. Establish a good credit rating.
6. Start saving for retirement, even if the amounts are small.
7. Get at least one credit card in your name—and use it wisely.

8. Look into the costs and benefits of buying a home.
9. Maintain adequate medical, disability, and life insurance coverage.
10. Reassess your job. Are you in line for a promotion? How much do you expect to earn 5 years from now? Should you think about retraining or going back to school?
11. Take advantage of the fact that you can manage your money to meet your needs. No one needs to approve your decisions or agree with your approach.
12. Create your own financial independence. Don't rely on someone else to do it for you.

GETTING MARRIED: CREATING FINANCIAL BONDS

T he man of your dreams just popped the question. Now what?

Women (and men) usually have very romantic views about love and marriage. When you consider joining forces with that special someone, you think about what he looks like, how his jokes make you laugh, how you like his spontaneity. But do you ever think about who the beneficiary is on his insurance policy, if he's in debt, or whether he holds that beach house jointly with his brother or as a tenant-in-common?

Sometimes love *does* conquer all. But, in most cases, more than hearts and flowers are required to make a marriage work. You and your husband are, among other things, financial partners. And as such, you should both be willing to discuss with each other how you spend money, how you save money, and what your financial goals are. Ignoring this more practical side of your life—and focusing just on the love aspect of your union—may, in fact, cause serious marital conflicts. In our experience, we have found that collaboration on financial planning issues and other money matters can actually aid in maintaining marital harmony because it keeps the lines of communication open.

Before you say "I do," you and your husband-to-be should sit down to compare notes. What are your monthly expenses? What is your monthly income? What are your assets? Should you hold them separately, jointly, or in some combination of the two? Are you prepared for emergencies? What are your financial priorities? And so on. Financial planning can't guarantee a successful marriage, but it certainly is an integral part of a sound foundation.

Discussing Finances

When men and women enter into the serious phase of a relationship, they generally find out everything they can about one other. Which summer camp did you attend? What's your favorite ice cream flavor? Do you wear boxers or briefs? Is that your natural hair color? Sharing such details with each other helps build intimacy. But when the talk turns to money, most couples clam up. You want me to tell you how much I'm worth? Share with you how deeply I'm in debt? Letting your beloved peek at your financial statements, it seems, is the last great taboo. In general, we are not comfortable talking about our money. It seems to be our deepest secret.

As the two of you begin this partnership together, however, it's important that you be open about your finances. Do a little detective work, if you must, to find out what you're getting yourself into, financially speaking. We're not implying that you hire a private detective (although those agencies have been called upon more in recent years as couples meet through personal ads and the Internet). Simply open your eyes, and don't be afraid to ask questions about his current financial status *before* you slip that ring onto your finger. Your personal well-being and peace of mind are at stake. Even if you find out things you don't like about your prospective spouse, at least you will be prepared and forewarned. And, once you know your financial situation, you can take steps to make sure his financial issues don't haunt you later on.

Check Out His Financial History

You don't have to be Sherlock Holmes to understand the basics about your future husband's financial situation. Find out about the following:

- What exactly does he do? What type of job does he have? Is he self-employed or employed by a firm or a company? What is his position? What are his professional goals? How stable is his situation?
- How much does he earn (roughly)? How is he compensated? Does he get paid on a weekly or monthly basis? Does he receive a bonus? Is his income based on commissions?
- How much debt does he owe? Does he seem worried about creditors? When he uses his credit card, is it returned routinely because it isn't "going through"?
- Does he own a house? Is there a mortgage? Second mortgage? Who is liable? Whose name is the title in? (This could be important if his ex-wife still owns half the house.)
- If he was married before, does he pay alimony and/or child support? If so, how much? For how long is he obligated to make those payments? Is he obligated to pay alimony and/or child support but failing to do so? That could impact your joint financial situation later on.
- Has he ever filed for bankruptcy? What were the circumstances? How have his financial affairs been conducted since that time? What is his credit rating?
- Does he own his own business? If so, how does he handle his books? Is he meticulous with his record-keeping? Aggressive in his tax positions? Are there liabilities associated with the business? Is the business incorporated or a partnership? How much money or capital does he expect to reinvest in the business each year?
- What are his family relationships? What financial position are his parents in, for instance, compared to him? Do they depend on him for financial support now, or do they expect him to support them in the future? Can his income support these obligations?
- What money does he have saved for retirement? Does he contribute regularly? Is he eligible for a pension?

Hopefully, you'll determine that he "checks out." The important point is to avoid surprises and know what you're getting into. Armed with an understanding of your sweetheart's financial situation, it's time to begin talking about how you each handle money. Everyone has at least slightly different attitudes toward money—what it means, how to use it, and the like. Spouses often have different expectations about how they should earn, save, and spend money together. Perhaps you like to spend money, and he prefers to save more. Or, you may want to invest money conservatively; he may feel more comfortable with a higher level of investment risk. It is normal for differences of opinion and style to exist between couples, especially when it comes to money. Significant problems arise, however, when the couple can't resolve those differences.

Reconciling two different money philosophies can be a challenge. But it needn't sound the death knell for an impending marriage. How should you deal with the situation? First, you and your fiancé should determine your financial objectives, short-, medium-, and long-term. Each of you should draw up your own list; then compare your responses. For example, in the short term you may want to pay off your credit card debt and for the medium term you may want to quit your job and stay at home to raise a family. Your husband's short-term objective, on the other hand, may be to buy a car. His medium-term goal may be to diversify his portfolio.

Next, you must ask yourselves: Are our objectives the same? If not, how can we compromise and still meet our goals? You may need to do some actual calculations to see if your goals are realistic. Could you really afford to give up your salary, for instance? If you run the real numbers—either by hand using a spreadsheet or on the computer with some financial planning software—it may help you reconcile your different objectives by giving you a more realistic financial picture. (See Chapter 1 for a budget worksheet.)

Your E&Y Planner Says:

When the two of you share your hopes and dreams for the future, you should be talking about financial planning to help make them come true.

PAYING THE BILLS

Getting married means that you and your husband will now be combining your finances (to some degree, of course). How you combine them is a critical issue. You need to think about how you'll pay for daily living expenses such as food, utilities, and the rent or mortgage. Some couples pool all of their money into one account, typically a joint checking account, from which they pay all of their bills. The advantage to this system is that it's very straightforward: Only one account needs to be maintained.

The disadvantage is that you can easily lose track of your balance—and possibly overdraw the account—because both you and your spouse will be writing checks, making ATM withdrawals, and so on, and you may forget to tell each other about payments that you've made. If only one spouse handles the checkbook, you won't run into this trouble, but you may have another problem. It's not a good idea for one spouse to turn over responsibility for—and thus, control of—the couple's finances to the other partner. Both you and your husband should understand your joint finances. Even if your husband handles all the bills and other paperwork, you should sit down with him each month and review his records. You need to know what's going on—even if you're not responsible for writing out the checks each month—because you may have to take over this task by yourself someday if your husband needs to be away for an extended period of time on business or in the military, if he becomes disabled or dies, or if you get divorced or your roles in the household change.

Alternatively, you and your husband could set up three separate accounts: yours, mine, and ours. You would pay your personal bills from your own account. Your husband would pay his personal bills from his account. And you both would contribute to the "ours" account and pay for joint purchases and expenses from that account. Many couples like this system because it allows them both to be involved in the family's financial matters, yet it gives both partners some mad money to spend as they wish without having to consult the other partner.

The drawback is that you may not have as much control over your finances as you do with the one-account system. How much money do you have in all three accounts, for instance? At any given moment, you simply may not know. Also, it's easy for resentment to build with this type of setup because you may feel that you are paying for a larger chunk of the family's expenses while your husband is free to spend his money on whatever he wishes. To make this method work, you must consider how much income each partner makes and then divide variable and fixed expenses accordingly.

A Case Study: Handling Bills and Expenses

When Jackie and Jordan married 10 years ago, they had a very modest income, so they decided to pool their resources. Shortly after their marriage, they set up joint savings and checking accounts. Each partner was free to write checks from the account for purchases. Jackie, however, soon found herself designated as the unofficial family bill-payer. Each month she would write checks to cover the telephone, electric and gas, rent, medical, and credit card bills. Afterward, she felt there was no money left to buy the things that she wanted. It seemed as though her entire salary disappeared into the mutual savings pool.

Jordan, on the other hand, never felt this pressure. He had a laissez-faire attitude about money management. He bought what he wanted, whenever he wanted. He never thought about budgeting or saving.

Fortunately, Jordan wasn't extravagant, so it's not as though he was putting the couple into debt. But, as a single woman, Jackie had always managed her own money very well. It had given her a sense of independence and autonomy. Jackie began to feel that she had no control over her money anymore. And it was beginning to affect her relationship with Jordan.

That's when Jackie came to see me. I reviewed the couple's cash flow. Jackie had actually done quite well managing their modest income. Although they were many years from retirement at the time, Jackie and Jordan were saving through their jobs and making small monthly deposits into Roth IRAs. They also had been able to save enough money to build a small vacation home in the mountains. They had an emergency fund that equaled 6 months' living expenses.

My advice was simple. Set up three separate savings and checking accounts. Label one *Jackie,* one *Jordan,* and the other *Ours.* The couple decided what percent of their incomes would go directly into the joint accounts, which would cover mutual expenses such as the rent, food, utilities, and insurance. They would continue to put some savings into a mutual account for vacations and big-ticket purchases. The remainder of their paychecks would go into their separate accounts, which they could then spend (or save) as they wished.

The result? Jackie no longer felt she carried the financial burdens of the household. "It may not be the most efficient way to handle our double income," she says. "But it gives me a sense of independence and accomplishment."

➤
Your E&Y Planner Says:

Does your husband make more money than you do? If so, will financial matters be decided jointly, or will he decide how the money should be spent? We have seen cases where the husband makes more money—or all the money—and he is the one to decide if he wants a boat, a car, or a new house. He may buy his wife gifts and jewelry as her "bonus," but, quite often, it's on his terms. This type of unequal partnership happens a lot more than we like to admit. If you find yourself in this situation and are not comfortable with this, you must act affirmatively to change it.

SETTING UP A SAVINGS PLAN

You and your spouse should set up a savings plan *together*. It will strengthen your financial partnership, give you more choices throughout your married life, and bring financial security. And, short of winning the lottery, saving money is the way most married couples reach their financial goals. It's important that you agree on a savings strategy, though. If one partner pushes the other into a particular savings plan, it will probably backfire.

Your chances of success are greater if you find a method that works for both of you. Start by thinking of saving as simply a decision to spend your money later. It's *not* a money diet. You'll still have money to buy things and generally enjoy life—but you won't be wasting money. And you'll have the funds needed in the future to buy a home, start a family, retire early, or accomplish whatever goals you and your spouse set your sights on.

One way to begin a savings plan is to arrange for automatic withdrawals from your checking account into a savings or investment account. This forces you to "pay yourself first" and create a disciplined savings plan. You and your spouse should agree on the percent you will save. You might also want to set up a separate savings or investment account for each of your major goals. For a short-term goal, such as saving for a ski trip, you can deposit funds into a money market account. For a long-term goal, such as retirement, a portfolio of various stock and bond mutual funds might be the right choice.

To track and control day-to-day spending, you and your spouse-to-be should agree on a weekly allowance for small daily needs. This will help curb impulse spending, which will allow you to make smarter decisions about how your money gets spent. You will also need to monitor your credit card spending. Both you and your intended probably had separate credit card accounts prior to the marriage. By all means, keep at least one account in your name. It's important to maintain your own credit history—in your own name—because you might need it later on if your husband dies or if you get divorced. Be careful, though. Newly married couples commonly get themselves into debt by overspending on the numerous credit cards that seem to pop into their mailboxes every day. Curbing credit card spending can be especially difficult when you are setting up a new joint household and you need to buy furniture, lamps, dishes, and so forth. One helpful hint: Before you buy any item, determine if it's a need or just a want.

Go over the items each of you already owns and agree on which ones you can use until you can comfortably afford to pick out new things together. This can also help you avoid purchasing mistakes. Being able to choose items together after you are married helps to keep the emotional and financial partnership healthy and on track. (See Chapter 1 for some sound advice on establishing credit and how to use credit cards.)

Your E&Y Planner Says:

You may want to establish a separate account to fund sudden impulses like a spur-of-the-moment weekend trip or some other purchase. If you had mad money when you were single, continue to budget for it now that you're married. It will keep life from feeling stale.

As a married pair you will also need a contingency fund (or financial cushion) to cover the costs of unanticipated events. If you have been planning carefully, you've probably had such a fund on your own, but now you must revise how much you will need in that fund based on increased costs and expectations of additional income. Your balance can be thrown off by unemployment, a sudden disability, or an unexpected home repair. Perhaps your job or your husband's will be downsized, and one of you will be unemployed for 3 months. Or maybe your roof will develop a leak or your car's transmission will need to be replaced. All of these situations are generally unplanned, and as such they can't be covered by your monthly budget. That's why you need an emergency cash reserve set aside for just this purpose. Most financial advisors suggest that your contingency fund equal at least 3 to 6 months of expenses, if possible. That amount should be enough to tide you over through emergencies or brief periods of unemployment.

Accounts appropriate for a contingency fund should be completely liquid—for instance, a passbook savings account, a money market mutual fund, or an interest-bearing checking account. Your funds should be safe from the fluctuations of the stock and bond markets, and you should be able to make withdrawals on short notice. Check-writing privileges and no early withdrawal penalties are a plus. And you should be earning an interest rate or an investment rate of return equal to or higher than the current inflation rate so you don't lose purchasing power on the amount in your contingency account.

Another quick and easy way to secure needed funds during an emergency is through an approved credit line. You can accomplish this by setting up, in advance, a home equity line of credit on your home or a sizable credit line on your credit card. Bear in mind that this strategy can cost you more in interest payments than simply withdrawing funds held in a contingency account.

> ### Your E&Y Planner Says:
>
> As you prepare to marry, you should also think about your retirement savings plans. You and your husband should continue to contribute to your respective plans if a 401(k) or similar plan is offered through your employer or if you've set up a SEP/IRA or a similar plan on your own. In theory, it makes some sense to take the most advantage of the plan in which the employer matches the 401(k)

contribution. But, as a woman, you need to protect yourself. You want to maximize both your husband's and your own retirement assets to the greatest extent possible. However, think twice about forgoing contributions into your own plan and pumping the maximum into his plan simply because his employer matches funds. Not that you plan for divorce, of course, but money in your own name is always preferable to counting on a settlement that allocates a portion of your spouse's retirement plan to you. Likewise, you shouldn't "balance" your retirement plans by putting all of your savings into conservative, lower-earning investments while your husband puts his savings into riskier, higher-earning ones. Each spouse's retirement plan should be a balance of investments. Otherwise, you will have a smaller nest egg to draw on in the future.

THE PRENUPTIAL AGREEMENT

Since nearly half of all first marriages in the United States are likely to end in divorce, more and more couples are deciding how they'll divide up their assets—before they say "I do." One way to protect yourself is to draw up a binding prenuptial agreement.

Prenuptial agreements (or *prenups*) are legal contracts that specify—before your marriage—who will pay for which expenses and how assets will be divided in case of divorce or death. Some prenups also lay ground rules for a marriage, noting, for instance, the city in which the couple will live and how many children they expect to raise. One couple in Albuquerque, New Mexico, actually spelled out in their prenuptial agreement how tidy they'd keep their home and how frequently they'd have sex together. (You probably will not want to go that far!)

Prenups cannot determine all the terms of a marriage, however. While you can outline in a prenuptial agreement the overall support terms that you think will be advisable in the case of divorce, a judge will ultimately decide what's in the best interest of the family if you and your spouse can't agree. Similarly, you can't waive child support payments in a prenuptial agreement. A wife can waive her right to alimony in a prenup (if she is earning a good salary, for instance, and doesn't see a need for alimony). From an emotional perspective, you may prefer a property settlement to receiving (or sending) a check each month.

These types of agreements are much more commonplace now than they were in the past. Men and women are marrying later in life; consequently, both the groom and the bride may have accumulated a home, a car, a retirement nest egg, and other assets in their own names. (That's a far cry from most couples in their 20s, who don't own much more than their wedding gifts when they marry.) In this case, a prenup can simply clarify who owns what before the marriage begins so there's less room for misunderstanding later. Should a misunderstanding develop in later years, at least you have a legal document that indicates where things stand.

More second and third marriages take place now, too, which means that you or your spouse may have children and assets from a previous marriage. A prenuptial agreement can ensure that your children—and not your current husband or his children—will eventually inherit your assets or that portion you have set aside for them.

In addition, a prenup can designate to what degree future assets will be shared or kept separate (see Figure 2.1). That could be important if you currently have assets from which you expect to generate a lot of income. It's also important if you expect a substantial increase in your income as a result of a promotion or a great new job, or because your business really takes off.

FIGURE 2.1   DIVISION OF ASSETS IN A PRENUPTIAL AGREEMENT

Some options that can determine how future assets will be shared or kept separate include:

1. Your or his premarital assets, including income and appreciation, remain separate.
2. Pre-marriage values of assets remain separate, including appreciation. All income on those assets is shared equally or pro rata.
3. All assets and income are pooled. Future income and appreciation is shared in an allocation set up in this document.
4. Only a portion of each partner's income is shared. Everything else is kept separate.

Many young couples still shy away from prenups, mostly because they can imply a lack of commitment and trust. Marriage is supposed to be a joint effort, after all, not a division of property. Too much discussion about what's yours, mine, and ours can make a young couple feel like they are getting divorced before they're even married.

Your E&Y Planner Says:

No matter how practical you are—even if you're drawing up a prenup at your parents' insistence because they want to protect the family assets—it's impossible to take all of the emotion out of a prenuptial agreement. You are planning for the possibility of death or divorce, after all, and either you or your prospective husband is bound to feel slighted in some real or imagined way. That's why we tell clients to think of a prenup as a marital insurance policy. Marriage is, among other things, a financial partnership. Addressing and dealing with practical issues early in the relationship may actually "insure" that the marriage survives. If not, at least you can be confident that your interests and assets will be protected over the long run. You may also discover that you just cannot agree on the terms of the prenuptial agreement. You might take that as a sign that there are flaws in the relationship.

 Men want prenuptial agreements. Women don't.

This common misperception stems from the notion that bread-winning husbands want to prevent the loss of assets should a marriage fail, while stay-at-home wives only want to see how much they can get. The reality is that either the husband or the wife may have assets coming into the marriage that he or she wants protected.

You Need a Prenup If . . .

You should consider getting a prenuptial agreement if you and/or your prospective husband:

- Have a lot of assets
- Have children from a previous marriage
- Have significantly more earning power than the other
- Own a business
- Have serious prospects of success, for example, as a bestselling author or a movie actor
- Enjoy a recognizable name in your field
- Are partners in a partnership
- Have ongoing familial obligations, including parents or other relations
- Have significant or potential future liabilities

Without a prenuptial agreement, you are letting your fate be determined by a third party should you and your husband eventually divorce and not be able to agree on a settlement you both believe is fair. If you don't have a prenup—and if you can't agree during the divorce proceedings on who gets the antique armoire and the new sound system—your assets will be divided according to the laws of the state in which you live. In community property states (Arizona, California, Idaho, Louisiana, Nevada, New Mexico, Texas, Washington, and Wisconsin), which generally view both spouses as equal owners of all marital or "community" property, you may get half of your marital assets. In equitable distribution states (that's the remaining states), property will ultimately be divided by the court, depending upon the number of years you were married, whether assets were purchased jointly, and several other considerations. (For a fuller discussion of divorce issues, see Chapter 6.) In most cases, you should get some share of the wealth accrued during your marriage—even if you stayed at home to raise a family while your husband built his business up—unless you have a prenuptial agreement that states otherwise.

Most prenuptial agreements will stand up in a court of law—provided you've taken certain precautions. If you draw up the document on the eve of your nuptials, your husband could argue later on that he signed under duress and the prenup could be ruled invalid. Similarly, an agreement may be considered invalid if the ultimate distribution of assets appears grossly unfair. Let's say, for instance, that you had $1 million going into the marriage, while your husband had $50,000. If, under the agreement, you walk away with $2 million when the marriage ends 10 years later while your husband's assets have been depleted to $30,000, that might appear to be grossly unfair and would probably be reason enough to disallow the prenuptial agreement.

In some prenuptial agreements, a spouse's rights increase if the marriage lasts a set number of years. For example, Harry will provide 25% of his annual income in alimony to Sheila if the marriage lasts more than 3 years but less than 5; 35% if more than 5 years but less than 10, and so on. In some cases a "sunset date" of, say, 20 years of marriage is offered, at which time the prenup automatically expires.

Spouses also have the option of *burning* the prenup earlier than the sunset date if desired. Even if the prenup said that Sheila was entitled to none of Harry's assets and only a stated alimony, Harry could always gift assets to Sheila at any time. These gifts wouldn't be returned in the event of a divorce or death.

Having a prenup won't necessarily save you all the expense and emotional upheaval of a full-fledged divorce. That's true especially if the parting is not amicable and either you or your husband are ready to fight for as much as you can get. But in many instances, a prenup can simplify an emotionally charged situation because it dictates how assets are split and what, if any, support payments are to be made.

To make sure your agreement is airtight, it's best to consult a respected family law or matrimonial lawyer. (Ask friends and relatives for a recommendation or consult *Best Lawyers in America,* a reference book available in most libraries.) Your attorney should be well versed in matrimonial issues relevant to the state in which you will be married and also the state in which you plan to live (if they are different). It's often helpful for the attorney to have knowledge of estate planning issues as well, since this is a good time for both you and your spouse to make sure that your estate plans are in order. (For more information on estate planning for couples, see Chapter 3.)

To prevent any claims of partiality later on, you and your fiancé should each seek separate legal counsel. This will ensure that both your interests and those of your future husband are being protected and represented fairly. If you both decide to use the family attorney, however, one of you must be the primary client. The other must sign a release stating that he or she chose not to seek outside counsel so that the validity of the prenup can't be challenged at a later date.

Once a prenup is drawn up and signed, it generally stands as is. If your financial situation changes dramatically—or if you've had a change of heart—you can create an *antenuptial agreement* that modifies or changes provisions of the original prenuptial contract. Similarly, if you didn't make an agreement before you married, you may be able to get one after you've said "I do." Valid in many states, such as New York and Illinois, these *postnuptial agreements* are akin to separation agreements—except you and your husband don't separate. With a prenuptial agreement, though, the consideration for the contract is the marriage itself. With a postnuptial contract, there is no inducement to sign—except a possible reconciliation, if your marriage is not going smoothly. A will can always supersede the prenuptial agreement and allocate assets to the spouse, even if under the prenuptial agreement the spouse is entitled to nothing.

A CASE STUDY: SECOND MARRIAGES AND PRENUPTIAL AGREEMENTS

It had been 2 years since Diane's husband, Jim, had died suddenly of a heart attack. After Jim's death, Diane spent most of her time working as an executive at a large corporation and raising her 8-year-old daughter, Bonnie, alone. She had no time to date. Until she met Rick, age 53, through a mutual friend. Rick had been divorced for several years and was the father of three children, ages 15, 20, and 21. Diane and Rick planned to marry in the coming months.

Money had never been an issue with Diane and her first husband. She had made more money than he had, but things just seemed to work out on their own. Now, Diane had an annual income of $200,000; owned a large suburban house worth $300,000; owned $10,000 worth of jewelry, which Jim had inherited from his mother and given to Diane when they were married; and amassed close to $200,000 in her 401(k) plan. She had also received $500,000 from Jim's life insurance, most of which she invested in various mutual funds.

Rick had done similarly well (or so Diane thought). He was an attorney with his own firm and several employees. At present, Rick's income was comparable to Diane's but, unlike Diane's stable salary, his income tended to fluctuate with the rise and fall of the stock market. In addition to his alimony payments, he was still making child support payments and was obligated by his divorce agreement to pay half of his children's college tuition. Even with these responsibilities, Rick talked of retiring before age 60. His Keogh plan was worth $250,000 but his overall net worth was less than $400,000. Because his two oldest children were away at college and his youngest child lived with his ex-wife, Rick rented a small two-bedroom apartment. Diane's parents had died a few years before; Rick's parents, however, lived close by and counted on him for emotional and financial support.

When the couple announced their engagement, Diane's close friends advised her to draw up a prenuptial agreement. Diane was reluctant at first, but soon realized that she had substantial assets to protect in case of divorce. In addition, she had to make sure Bonnie would be taken care of.

Diane cautiously broached the subject of a prenup to Rick a few months before the wedding. Fortunately, he welcomed the idea because he realized that he had to protect his own children. So the couple met with me one afternoon. I recommended that their prenuptial agreement address the following issues:

1. *Residence.* Will Diane and Rick live in Diane's house or will they buy a house together?
2. *Wills.* The agreement should require that both Diane and Rick execute new wills after the marriage and should lay out the provisions of those wills. Should Diane die without a will after her marriage, Rick would inherit a substantial portion of her estate under state law. I recommended that the prenup state that Rick should be entitled to very little upon Diane's death. (Under most state laws, a spouse must be left something in your will.) But, if Diane wishes, the law allows her to be more generous when the actual will is drafted. The initial will may leave everything to Bonnie, but Diane

can always amend the document in favor of Rick if she wants to make sure he is taken care of in later years when Bonnie is more independent, or if she wants to take advantage of the marital deduction to save estate taxes.

3. *Long-term care insurance.* Although Rick is in good health, the prenuptial agreement should require that he obtain long-term care insurance for both himself and his parents to provide for nursing home costs that might be incurred if any of them got sick. Since Diane and Rick would be unable to qualify for Medicaid because their net worth as a couple would be beyond the income limitations, Diane would be forced to support Rick in the absence of long-term care insurance, possibly jeopardizing her own financial independence.

4. *Divorce.* The agreement should detail what happens in case of divorce. Does either partner want alimony? If they buy a house together, who gets it after the divorce? Do they want to provide for any type of property settlement?

5. *Household expenses.* I suggested that Diane and Rick discuss now how they plan to share the costs of their joint household. Rick wants to retire early. How does he plan to support himself? To protect her own financial independence, Diane may want to state in the agreement that Rick is responsible for funding his own retirement and that she is not to be solely responsible for all their expenses.

6. *Support of Rick's parents and children.* The prenup should also stipulate that Rick is solely responsible for the support of his parents, including food, shelter, and medical care. Although Diane may care for his elderly parents, she may not want to be financially responsible for them. Rick's divorce agreement provides that he pay half of his kids' college tuition as well as monthly child support for his youngest. Diane needs to protect herself by having the agreement state that she is not liable for those obligations. However, if Rick's ex-wife petitions the court for additional child support after Rick marries Diane, the court may likely determine that Rick's disposable income has increased and may order him to pay more child support because Diane's contribution of her income to the household has freed up more of his money. If this should happen, the agreement can provide that Diane be compensated for any decrease in the amount that Rick is failing to contribute to their household.

7. *Retirement assets.* If Diane and Rick divorce, the agreement should provide that Diane's 401(k) account is not a marital asset and is exempt from equitable distribution. That will protect Diane upon divorce. But if she dies, Rick—and not Bonnie—would get the money in the 401(k) because under ERISA law, that money automatically goes to the spouse (unless the spouse has waived that right during married life). Even if Rick waived his right to Diane's 401(k) in the prenup, it wouldn't be effective and Rick would still get the money. So what can Diane do? The prenup can stipulate that Rick agrees to waive his right to the 401(k) after the couple marries. What if Rick decides he doesn't want to waive his rights after the honeymoon? Diane can sue him for breach of contract. Another option would be for the agreement to state that, if the waiver is not executed, any benefits Diane has provided for Rick in the prenup or her will are to be proportionately reduced by the amount in the 401(k) upon her death.

8. *Miscellaneous issues.* Whose health insurance will they use? Who will be the beneficiary of their life insurance policies—each other, their kids, a trust? Do Diane and Rick have disability insurance?

9. *Jurisdiction.* The agreement should specify the laws of the state that Diane and Rick want to apply in interpreting the prenup. In general, this is the state where they are residing upon execution. However, if they're thinking of relocating or retiring to another state, they should consider the impact of that state's laws on the agreement. A judge may disregard the jurisdiction provision if there is no connection with that state when the prenup is before the court.

10. *Power of attorney/health care proxy.* Does Diane want Rick, a close friend, or a relative to have a power of attorney over her assets if she is incapacitated? What kind of power of attorney should be executed—special, durable, or springing? Perhaps Rick could have power of attorney over their residence if they own it jointly, but not over Diane's separate assets. Does Diane feel comfortable naming Rick as the person to make her health care decisions if she is incapacitated? Diane may assume that she'll be named as health care proxy for Rick, but Rick may be more comfortable naming one of his children.

Before her wedding, Diane has a lot more to think about than picking a caterer and deciding what she'll wear.

If You Marry a Man of Modest Means . . .

Let's assume you have minimal assets, too. What should you do? Plan now. Look closely at your assets, your liabilities, and your cash flow. Would either of you consider working a second job or going back to school so that you can get a better-paying job? Where can you economize? In many ways, the old adage that two can live as cheaply as one is true. But, you must find ways to make this happen. Curb your impulse spending. Start a savings plan—even if you can only afford to put away a minimal amount each month. Adopt a pay-as-you-go spending style instead of relying heavily on credit cards. You need some type of plan, or you'll never achieve financial independence as a couple.

If You Marry a Wealthy Man . . .

Assuming you don't have any money to speak of, you should continue to save on your own. Don't expect your husband—no matter how wealthy he is—to always provide for you. He can change his will at any time, and you could be left with far less than you expect (depending upon the laws of the state in which you live and how your assets are held in title). Have an attorney review your prenuptial agreement closely (if there is one). This document can't be changed as easily as a will, but it's getting harder to disprove their validity in court if you both signed willingly.

If you are a man's second or third wife, expect that he may be more reluctant to share his financial assets with each marriage. You, the latest wife, will get fewer assets in a prenuptial agreement than his earlier wives did. The elderly grandmother of one of my clients got an "allowance" from her husband. (She was wife number 3.) She was frugal, fortunately, and saved as much as possible. When the husband died, he left everything to his children—and nothing to her.

Another client admitted that she treated gifts of jewelry received from wealthy beaux as her retirement fund. When she got older—and needed money—she planned to sell off the pieces. That's not a bad idea, but a brokerage account may be a sounder financial move.

If You Marry Later in Life . . .

When you marry at an older age, you have a better idea of the kind of person you are marrying: Is he ambitious? Charitable? A corporate type or an entrepreneur? For the most part, his personality—and financial perspective—are formed. The older you are when you say "I do," though, the more likely it is that you'll be bringing some issues to the partnership. Do you have children—and, thus, future college tuitions to pay? Does he? Is your parents' health declining? Are you expected to care for them? What about his aging parents?

There's also the fairness issue. If you both have kids, and you receive child support, does that necessarily free up your and your new husband's joint funds to help care for his children? Unfortunately, these emotionally charged issues have no ready answers. Take time to discuss these issues with your soon-to-be spouse, because your decisions can seriously impact the financial and emotional well-being of your family unit and your future years.

LOOKING AHEAD:
What You Should Be Doing Right Now

1. *Check out your fiancé's financial background.* How much money does he earn? What debts does he owe? What investments does he have? Any business ventures or real estate holdings? Has he ever been bankrupt? Is he responsible for any alimony or child support payments? The answers to these basic questions should give you some sense of your intended's financial stability.
2. *Talk about money.* What's his saving and spending philosophy compared to yours? Opposites may attract, but differing spending styles can cause lots of friction and leave you holding debts. Once you're married, your credit rating is tied to his.
3. *Set up a saving plan.* Determine your joint financial goals. If necessary, pay yourself first with automatic monthly withdrawals from your checking account to a savings or investment account.

4. *Set up a spending plan.* Some couples pool their money into one account. Others use "yours," "mine," and "ours" accounts. Each system has its advantages and disadvantages. The one you choose should match your personal attitudes and needs.

5. *Review all documents.* If you don't have any children, it's likely that you named your parents, siblings, and/or other relatives as the beneficiaries on your life insurance policies and retirement plan assets. You'll probably want to make your husband the beneficiary as soon as you tie the knot. Make sure he does the same, if agreed.

6. *Review health care plans.* One spouse's health insurance may be preferable over the other's.

7. *Consult legal counsel.* Talk with an attorney about creating a prenuptial agreement. If it makes sense for you, work this out with your fiancé.

3

MARRIAGE: PLANNING AHEAD

Whether you are newlyweds or have just celebrated your silver anniversary, estate planning may be the furthest thing from your mind—and it is probably not a topic you enjoy discussing. But, at the very least, you and your husband should plan how much of your estate you and he want each other to receive in the event of death. In addition, you may need to plan carefully if one of you is financially dependent on the other. It is never too early or too late to make concrete plans for the distribution of assets that you will amass together or that you have already built up.

ESTATE PLANNING FOR COUPLES

The old maxim says that nothing is certain in life except death and taxes. Effective estate planning can help you prepare for both eventualities. The difficulty with estate planning, however, is that it forces people to think about their own mortality—and, if you're like most people, you are not eager to address these issues. But making the necessary preparations now will ensure that you and your family will be provided for and forestall unnecessary hassles.

■ 59

The Will

A will (formally known as a *last will and testament*) specifies who will inherit your property, names a guardian for minor children, and designates an executor who will handle your financial affairs after you die. Any citizen of the United States 18 years of age or older can have a will. If you change your mind about the provisions of your will, you can always change your will or simply add an amendment, known as a *codicil.* You're permitted to draft an unlimited number of wills and codicils, as long as each document is signed by you, dated, and witnessed according to your state's laws.

If you die intestate—that is, without a will—your assets will be distributed according to state law, regardless of your wishes. In many states, a married woman's assets pass directly to her husband if she dies without a will. For some couples that distribution may be the arrangement they would have chosen anyway. Still, it's best to have the disposition of your assets protected (legally) by a will. Consider this situation: You and your husband are in a car accident. Neither of you has children, and neither has a will. You die immediately; your husband dies a few weeks later. Since you die first, all of your assets go to your husband. When your husband dies, all of his assets—including what he inherited from you—will go to his parents (if living). That means your antique dining table won't go to your sister who has always admired it and your investments won't go to your retired parents. Instead, your husband's belongings—and yours—go to your in-laws. Is this what you want?

It's also crucial to execute a will if your estate is substantial. In general, in 1999, federal estate tax is incurred on taxable estates worth $650,000 or more; the amount will grow to $1 million by 2006. After the exemption amount, the estate and gift tax rate is 37% and goes up to 55%. Because of the 55% rate, failing to have a proper estate plan in place can result in Uncle Sam receiving more than your family does for very large estates.

To save on estate taxes, couples often set up trusts. For example, a bypass trust, which is commonly used, ensures that married couples take advantage of each spouse's *unified estate and gift tax credit.* Here's how it works:

Upon your death, you can leave up to $650,000 worth of property (in 1999) to your children, friends, or family members—and you won't owe any estate tax since each person is entitled to a lifetime federal *uni-*

fied estate and gift tax credit (referred to as the unified credit) of $211,300, which is equivalent to the tax that would be owed on a gift of $650,000. (This $650,000 amount is referred to as the *applicable exclusion amount.*) In other words, federal estate and/or gift taxes will not be assessed on the first $650,000 of combined taxable gifts and transfers at death.

As a wife, however, you can also leave as much as you want to your spouse (as long as he is a U.S. citizen) during your lifetime or when you die—without incurring any estate tax. That's called the *unlimited marital deduction.* If you left all of your assets to your husband using the *unlimited marital deduction,* there would be no estate taxes paid when you die. This sounds like a good plan, but for estates greater than $650,000, it may not be. Why? You did not use your unified estate and gift tax credit, and it doesn't carry over after your husband's death. That means the entire amount of your and your husband's assets would be included in the estate of the second to die.

When the surviving spouse dies, the heirs would pay estate taxes on those assets. However, you could avoid estate taxes when the first spouse dies—and still pay no estate taxes when the surviving spouse dies—with an alternate plan. Establish a family trust in your will and direct that it be funded with assets equal to the *applicable exclusion amount.* (In 1999, that amount is $650,000.) The remainder of your estate would then pass to your spouse, estate tax free, under the *marital deduction.* When your spouse died, the trust assets would pass to your heirs, estate tax free. Your spouse could bequeath his remaining assets (up to $650,000 in 1999) tax free to those heirs using the unified credit. This is called a *bypass trust* because it allows the assets to bypass taxation in the surviving spouse's estate.

It may appear that your husband is worse off under this arrangement, but the trust can be structured to provide him with virtually all the benefits he would have received if your assets had passed directly to him. Your will can provide that your husband act as trustee of the trust, giving him the power to manage the assets. In addition, he can receive all the income the trust earns and can have access to the principal for health, education, maintenance, and support reasons.

Whether you and your husband have substantial assets, a moderate estate, or little more than your wedding gifts, you should address these three basic issues in your will:

1. Whom Will You Name as Executor? The executor is responsible for the distribution of your assets according to the provisions of your will. In addition, the executor's duties include paying your debts, funeral bills, and taxes; claiming your life insurance; notifying your creditors; and selling your property, if necessary. Many married couples name the surviving spouse as executor and one or more of their adult children as successor executor(s). However, being an executor can be a complex and time-consuming job, especially for large estates. Check with the person you wish to name as executor to see if he or she wants the job. For large estates, it may be advisable to name a third party, such as a bank or an attorney, as executor or co-executor to ensure that the correct actions are taken and conflicts between heirs are minimized.

2. Who Will Receive Your Property? Your will states to whom you want to leave your assets (the recipients are referred to as *beneficiaries*), and how much they get. When you designate a beneficiary, clearly identify the recipient (such as "my brother, Joe Smith") and describe the asset in detail (such as "my red 1998 convertible").

Most people think that a will dictates who will receive all their property when, in fact, some or most of their property may pass outside a will. Your will dictates the recipient of your probate assets only. Your nonprobate assets, such as assets titled "joint with right of survivorship," assets with a designated beneficiary (such as life insurance and retirement plans), and assets held in trust, are not governed by your will.

Assets titled jointly with right of survivorship will automatically pass to the surviving joint tenant regardless of the terms of your will. Many people hold their homes, checking accounts, and investments jointly with their spouses. If for tax purposes or some other reason you don't want your interest in joint property to pass automatically to the surviving joint tenant, you should change your ownership of the property to "tenants-in-common" (where you each own one-half) or to one spouse's name alone.

If you hold all assets as joint with rights of survivorship, you will not have any assets to pass into the bypass trust established under your will. The result could be hundreds of thousands of dollars of additional estate taxes when your husband dies.

Similarly, assets such as your life insurance policies and retirement plans will pass to the beneficiary regardless of the terms of your will. For this reason, make sure that your beneficiary designations are current. You may have named your parents as beneficiaries of your company-provided life insurance when you started working, for example. If you fail to change the beneficiary designations before you die, the life insurance proceeds will pass to your parents even if you specifically state in your will that you want them to pass to your husband. That could be a financial disaster if your husband was depending on those funds for his continued support. By law, however, your retirement assets must generally go directly to your spouse unless he consents to a different beneficiary.

Be sure to review and update your beneficiary designations periodically. Clearly, the birth of a child or a divorce signals that you must change those designations. But married couples without children need to think about changes involving friends and other family members.

3. What Happens If You Are Disabled or Unable to Act on Your Own? At the same time you execute your will, you should execute three other equally important documents: a durable power of attorney, a health care power of attorney, and a living will. A durable power of attorney grants authority to one or more individuals to manage your financial affairs on your behalf if you are disabled or aren't capable of managing your finances yourself. You can create a power of attorney on a temporary or a long-term basis. Some states allow you to sign a "springing" power of attorney: one that springs into effect when you are disabled.

Living wills (sometimes called directives to physicians) and durable health care powers of attorney (sometimes called health care proxies or medical powers of attorney) are similar documents for health care. Their purpose is to make sure that your wishes regarding health care issues are carried out. A living will is a statement that lets you specify your wishes about being kept alive by extraordinary artificial life support equipment. A health care power of attorney appoints a person to make medical and health care decisions on your behalf in the event of your temporary or permanent incapacity.

The Best Place to Store a Will

Many people store their wills in their safe deposit boxes. But that isn't the best place. In many states, safe deposit boxes are sealed upon the death of the box's renter. And that can prove problematic and costly. Upon your death, your original will must be filed with the Register of Wills to begin the probate process. (See Chapter 7 for a detailed discussion of probate.) But if your will is stored in a box that's sealed when you die, the probate process will be delayed and it may be costly to have the box opened. (Either your attorney or the estate's executor needs authorization from the probate court to open up the box.) It's best to store the original document with your attorney. You and your spouse should keep copies of your wills in your safe deposit box and in a safe place at home.

A CASE STUDY: IN EACH OTHER WE TRUST

Pamela and Stephen, a happily married couple, had executed their wills almost a decade ago. But Pamela was growing concerned. She had been convinced, upon the advice of her husband and her attorney, that—to save on estate taxes—most of the couple's joint assets should not pass directly to the surviving spouse. Rather, those assets should be put into trusts created by their wills.

Sadly, Stephen had been recently diagnosed with cancer. Pamela was having second thoughts about the trusts. She was worried that she wouldn't be able to make ends meet if all of her money was tied up in a trust. That's when the couple came to see me.

I reviewed Pamela and Stephen's financial information as well as their wills. Stephen had named Pamela as the beneficiary of his life insurance policies and his retirement plans. All of the couple's investments were titled jointly. As a result, very few assets were actually going to be transferred to the trust created in Stephen's will. The trust provisions offered Pamela many benefits. She would receive the annual income earned by the trust assets and, as trustee, she could withdraw as much of the trust principal as she needed for her health, education, maintenance, and support. Pamela soon agreed that assets placed in the trust were just as beneficial to her as they would be if they had been transferred directly to her.

The couple needed to make some changes, however, if they wanted to minimize their estate tax bill. The first was that each should fund the trusts created under their wills with assets equal to the applicable exclusion amount. (In 1999, that amount is $650,000.) The best way to do that was for both Stephen and Pamela to change the designated beneficiaries for their separate life insurance policies from each other to the trust. The proceeds of their policies ($470,000 each), therefore, would go into their respective trusts.

Then we looked at the funding of Stephen's trust.

- First, we have the $470,000 from his insurance policy.
- This leaves $180,000 needed in order to fund the full $650,000 credit amount.
- Next, we look at other assets. Pamela and Stephen jointly own mutual funds worth $200,000.
- If they title $160,000 of these assets in Stephen's name, he can leave this amount to the trust.
- The ownership of the remaining $40,000 can be changed from joint tenants to tenants-in-common. Unlike the situation in joint tenancy, assets held as tenants-in-common do not automatically pass to the spouse. Stephen's $20,000 can also pass to the trust.
- By doing this, Stephen has funded the trust with the entire amount. The summary of trust funding is as follows:

    $470,000—life insurance

    $160,000—mutual funds in Stephen's name

    $ 20,000—Stephen's share of mutual funds held as tenants-in-common

Stephen died shortly after putting these plans in place. Pamela has been using the income the trust earns to meet her day-to-day living expenses, so she has not needed to withdraw any principal from the trust. Having a firm estate plan in hand didn't help Pamela prepare emotionally for her husband's death. But it did give her one less thing to worry about during the couple's last year together.

Trusts

There are two major types of trusts: testamentary trusts and living trusts. Testamentary trusts are funded when you die. Instead of leaving money directly to a beneficiary, you leave it in trust, to be managed by a trustee. Married couples often leave their money in a testamentary trust because:

1. A trust can hold money until a child grows up. You can indicate for what purpose the funds should be used, and when and how much the child should receive.
2. A trust can hold money left to a spouse. After your death, the trust could enable your surviving spouse to receive income from the trust, and, if needed, payments out of the principal. When your spouse dies, the remaining money goes to whomever is named beneficiary. If the trust is structured properly, you can assure that your children will receive an inheritance if your spouse remarries.
3. A trust can also ensure that your children from a prior marriage will inherit your assets by preventing your second spouse from spending all of your money or bequeathing it to someone else. A trust can give your second spouse an income for life while guaranteeing that your children will ultimately inherit the remainder of your estate.

The trust arrangement married couples typically use to accomplish items 2 and 3 above is the qualified terminable interest property (QTIP) trust. The QTIP trust allows you (assuming you die before your husband) to decide who will ultimately inherit your estate. A QTIP trust gives a lifetime income to your husband after you die, but when your husband dies, the remaining principal in the trust passes on to whomever you have chosen. For most married couples, a QTIP trust protects the children from your current marriage: If your husband remarries and leaves all of his assets (including what you left to him) to his new wife, your children may be left with nothing. Similarly, a QTIP trust protects your children from a previous marriage: If you leave your estate outright to your second husband, he may not leave anything to the children from your first marriage. A QTIP trust differs from a bypass trust in that you can fund a QTIP trust with unlimited funds that qualify for the marital deduction. A bypass trust is typically limited to the amount of the exemption equivalent, which is $650,000 in 1999 (and will increase to $1 million in 2006). The QTIP trust, to the extent that it is greater than the amount of the credit, will be taxable.

Trusts, including QTIP trusts, can be set up and funded during your lifetime as well as at your death. Living trusts are set up and funded while you're alive. (These assets are non-probate property; that is, they do not go through probate before distribution to the beneficiaries.) Revocable living trusts can be amended or revoked by you at any time. Once you die, the trust becomes irrevocable. These trusts are used to avoid probate and/or provide management of your property during your lifetime.

Revocable trusts do not save estate taxes. Since you still have control over the assets during your life, the assets are included in your estate and thus may be subject to estate tax when you die.

Irrevocable living trusts, however, cannot be changed once the trust is in place. Typically, irrevocable trusts are created to remove property and its future income and growth from your estate (and thus save estate taxes) as well as to control who becomes the ultimate beneficiary of those assets. You can deposit your life insurance policies into an irrevocable living trust, for instance, to save on estate taxes.

You should consider setting up a trust if you want to:

- Provide for your beneficiaries
- Reduce your estate taxes and income taxes
- Provide asset management
- Avoid probate

Owning Property Together

During your marriage, you and your husband will acquire property. It may be a home, one or more savings accounts, some investment accounts, perhaps art, and other assets. Many couples hold everything they own in joint names (joint with right of survivorship). Others take title as tenants-in-common. How you hold your property as a married couple will ultimately determine the amount of taxes incurred by your estates and whether or not a given asset must pass through probate (see Figure 3.1).

Joint Tenancy with Right of Survivorship

You and your husband own the property together. If he dies, you automatically get his share, and vice versa. Many married couples acquire assets this way without realizing that the result is that these assets will pass outside their wills. Often couples acquire a house under this arrangement simply because their real estate attorney assumed that's what they wanted.

FIGURE 3.1   HOW DOES PROPERTY PASS TO YOUR HEIRS? WILL IT GO THROUGH PROBATE?

Joint Tenancy with Right of Survivorship	$\rightarrow$		HEIRS
Revocable Trusts and Beneficiary Designations [IRAs, 401(k)s, etc.]	$\rightarrow$		HEIRS
Individually Owned Property	$\rightarrow$	PROBATE ESTATE	$\rightarrow$	HEIRS
Community Property	$\rightarrow$	PROBATE ESTATE	$\rightarrow$	HEIRS
Tenancy-in-Common	$\rightarrow$	PROBATE ESTATE	$\rightarrow$	HEIRS

The major drawback is that you can't fund a bypass trust (see the "Estate Planning" section in this chapter) with property that is held as joint with right of survivorship. Since state law dictates that property under this arrangement should pass directly to the joint tenant, there would be no property remaining with which to fund the trust.

Tenancy-in-Common

Married couples use this method if they want to leave their share of jointly owned property in trust. This arrangement gives spouses the same rights during their lifetimes. When you die, however, your share of the property does not automatically go to your husband. Instead, it passes to whomever you named as the beneficiary in your will. If you die without a will, your share of the property will be distributed according to the laws of the state in which you live. (In most cases, the recipient will be your spouse, if he's living.)

Tenancy by the Entirety

This arrangement is similar to property owned jointly with the right of survivorship—except you have a bit more protection. Neither you nor your spouse can divide the property without the other's consent. In some cases the property is protected against your spouse's creditors—if you didn't also sign the debt.

Community Property

Under the laws of the nine community property states (Arizona, California, Idaho, Louisiana, Nevada, New Mexico, Texas, Washington, and Wisconsin), nearly all property acquired by either you or your husband during the marriage is owned by both of you, regardless of whose name is on the deed. When moving to a new state, it is important not only to have your will reviewed by an attorney to determine whether your new state's laws require change but also to understand the property ownership laws of your new state. For example, if you move from a community property state to a common law (non-community property) state, you may not realize that when your husband opens a savings account and "for convenience" titles it in his name only, you have no right to that account.

Conversely, if you and your husband have agreed that the money you earn is yours and consequently you deposit your income into an account titled in your name only, moving from a common law state to a community property state will result in your husband owning one-half of your deposits plus one-half of the investment income earned on the entire account.

What can you do under these circumstances? In the first case, title the assets that you and your husband consider to be owned 50% by each as tenants-in-common or tenants by the entirety. In the second case, get your husband to agree (without duress, of course) to execute a postnuptial agreement. In most cases, you can circumvent the community property laws by executing a pre- or postmarital agreement. (See Chapter 2 for a complete discussion of pre- and postmarital agreements.)

Your E&Y Planner Says:

I recommend very limited use of joint property ownership. For estates where combined family assets don't exceed the unified credit exemption amount ($650,000 in 1999), unlimited use of jointly owned property generally causes few problems. For larger estates, however, I typically recommend that only your working bank account be held in joint names. You can receive all the benefits—and none of the additional estate tax—by titling assets as tenants-in-common.

A CASE STUDY: A TRUST BYPASSES TAXES

Mary and Jack have been married for 35 years. Jack's estate is worth $1 million; Mary's assets are worth $250,000. Both are concerned about estate planning. How can they provide the maximum amount for each other and the balance for their two children—without incurring substantial estate tax? That's what this couple wanted to know.

Jack and Mary assumed that they would leave all of their property to each other in their wills (called "I love you" or "sweetheart" wills). At first glance, this seemed like a smart strategy to them, so I explained what would happen if they made such arrangements. Since women typically outlive men, let's assume that Jack died first. No federal estate taxes would be incurred because the unlimited marital deduction would shelter the amount left to the surviving spouse from estate taxes (see Option 1 below). So far, so good. When Mary died, no federal estate taxes would be owed on the first $650,000 because of her unified credit. The next $650,000, however, would be subject to $258,500 in taxes. Why? Jack did not use his *unified credit* because he gave all of his assets to his wife under the *unlimited marital deduction.*

I told Jack and Mary that they could save that $258,500 if they set up a bypass trust rather than leaving all of their property to each other in their wills. Upon Jack's death, $650,000 would go to the bypass trust. No taxes would be due on this amount because Jack's unified credit would offset the taxes on the transfer. Jack's will would take advantage of the unlimited marital deduction by directing that the remaining amount in his estate pass directly to Mary. When Mary died, no estate taxes would be due on the amount in the bypass trust. And Mary's estate would pass entirely free of

OPTION I FULLY UTILIZING THE UNLIMITED MARITAL DEDUCTION		
	Jack	**Mary**
Estate	$1 million	$300,000
Marital deduction	($1 million)	$1 million
Taxable estate	0	$1,300,000
Estate tax	0	$469,800
Unified credit	0	$211,300
Estate taxes payable	0	$258,500

OPTION 2 FULLY UTILIZING UNIFIED CREDITS		
	Jack	**Mary**
Estate	$1 million	$300,000
Marital deduction	($355,000)	$355,000
Taxable estate	$650,000	$650,000
Estate tax	$211,300	$211,300
Unified credit	($211,300)	($211,300)
Estate taxes payable	0	0

estate taxes because of her unified credit (see Option 2). Not surprisingly, Mary and Jack decided to set up a bypass trust that very day.

INSURANCE PLANNING FOR COUPLES

As a single person, you may have had little or no life insurance—and rightly so. If you have no dependents and no debt, you don't need life insurance to replace your income when you die. Although you are now married, your life insurance needs may not have changed all that much. If you both work and if neither of you is dependent on the other for support, if you don't have any children, and if your husband could still live the same lifestyle without your salary, there's probably no reason to increase your life insurance coverage. Typically, there is no need to increase your coverage until you have or adopt a child. However, if your lifestyle changes such that your costs now require both of your paychecks, you and your husband may need to buy additional life insurance coverage. Often, married couples buy a bigger life insurance policy when they purchase a home together if one income cannot support the mortgage payments.

Disability insurance is an issue whether you are single or married, because it provides income in the event that you are injured or become seriously ill and cannot work. You have a much greater chance of being disabled than of dying if you're in your 30s or 40s. And being disabled can be quite expensive. Not only won't you be earning your weekly paycheck, but you will probably incur additional medical and rehabilitation expenses. This coverage is often best obtained through your employer or a professional trade association to reduce costs. (See Chapter 5 for more information.)

If both you and your husband are working, you probably get health insurance through your respective employers. Plans vary enormously in cost and in range of benefits offered. Often, you may be able to arrange it so that virtually all of your medical costs are covered—aside from deductibles and specific out-of-pocket costs—through coordination of benefits. (See Chapter 5 for a more detailed explanation.) If you anticipate that you and your husband will have some expenses that will not be covered under either plan, you may want to consider a benefit offered by some companies called a flexible spending account.

Here's how it works: You estimate your family's out-of-pocket health care expenses for the year. Your employer deducts that amount (up to a set maximum) from your pretax salary over the course of the year. That money is deposited into a special account from which all your out-of-pocket medical expenses can be reimbursed whenever you need cash to pay for a medical expense that's not covered by your insurance. (That includes deductibles and copayments.) The advantage is that you get a tax break: The income put into a flexible spending account isn't taxed. The drawback, however, is that you forfeit any money left in the account to the employer at year-end. The likelihood that you'll actually lose money with this arrangement is slim, however. If the year is ending and you have money left, you can go to the dentist, buy glasses, and so on. You can use the account for any medical expense considered tax deductible. This is a more liberal definition than most health insurance plans offer and will generally cover everything from contact lenses to birth control pills. Under the law, you can use up to the full amount you plan to set aside in a year before you've actually had it taken from your paycheck. If you leave your employment before the end of the year, you do not need to repay this money.

LOOKING AHEAD:
What You Should Be Doing Right Now

1. *Draw up a will.* In it, you name an executor and decide who gets your property and when.
2. *Consider a trust.* There are several different kinds. You can set up a trust for estate and income tax savings or for asset protection purposes.

3. *Understand ownership issues.* If you're buying a home or acquiring other substantial property together, be sure to understand how you and your husband hold title to the property.
4. *Review your insurance needs.* Make sure you're covered by disability insurance. Now that there are two of you, you might want to consider setting up a flexible spending account for out-of-pocket medical expenses.
5. *Review your beneficiary designations.* Make sure you update them to take into account your current situation.

4

LIVING TOGETHER

You've decided to move in together. Whether you're younger or older, divorced, widowed, or never married, or part of a same-sex couple or a heterosexual pair, your living together arrangement raises some new financial issues. Obviously, some of these matters will closely resemble the issues married couples face. (You might want to look at Chapters 2, 5, and 6 to see what applies to your particular situation.) As you may already know, however, many of the laws pertaining to married couples don't necessarily cover unmarried partners.

In this chapter we'll focus on the differences between being married versus living with someone without marriage. The length of the relationship doesn't really matter. Some issues will concern partners who have been together for years. Other issues will be equally relevant to those who have just begun a living together arrangement to "see how it goes."

The main drawback of a short-term living together relationship is that it may be difficult to decide how to combine (or even discuss) your finances without knowing whether this is a long-term commitment. The disadvantage of a serious, longer-term relationship, however, is that you may tend to treat your financial situation as though you were married, even though you don't have the protection that marriage often provides. Marriage is a legal, binding relationship that grants each partner some rights. Living together generally offers no such protection for either partner's assets or future standard of living.

If you're thinking of moving in with someone, consider these three important points:

1. *Protect yourself.* Many of the laws that automatically protect spouses don't apply to unmarried partners. Make sure that, in the event your partner dies or the two of you decide to separate, the assets you brought into the relationship—and/or purchased during the relationship—remain with you.

2. *Talk about money.* Discuss how you will pay your monthly expenses. Will you buy a home together? Open a joint checking account? Long-term partners—whether they're married or not—are apt to pool some of their funds. The longer you are together, the more entangled—and harder to split—those funds will be.

3. *Document your decisions.* You may have the best of intentions, but if you fail to write a will that makes it all legal, you or your partner could be left with nothing when either of you die. Also, make your plans known to other family members. Otherwise they might challenge some of the arrangements later on.

Combining Households

When you move in with someone who isn't legally your spouse, it's important to make a list of the items each of you is contributing to the new household. Include everything from your antique dining room table and matching chairs to that super-deluxe microwave oven. Such an inventory makes it clear, in the event that you separate or one of you dies, to which property each of you is entitled. You should keep an inventory with your will and other legal documents. You may want your attorney to keep a copy as well.

The same record-keeping procedure should apply to new purchases made after you've set up house together. If you buy a new television, and both of you contribute money toward the purchase, make sure you document the dollar amount contributed by each partner. Generally, if you pay for something, you own it. That means you can take the item with you if you separate or if your partner dies—unless you bought the item for your partner as a gift.

Too often, one partner foots the entire bill for, let's say, bedroom furniture. In the interest of maintaining a positive, trusting relationship with the other partner, however, that new four-poster bed and bureau are simply added to the household. No record is made of who bought, and thus owns, this property. It's only years later, when you are breaking up the household due to a separation or a death, that you are likely to fight over possession of these "undeclared" items. This may sound harsh, but remember that neither of you will have the benefit of a divorce settlement.

Paying Day-to-Day Expenses

Much like a newly married pair, an unmarried couple also needs to consider how they will pay for their daily living expenses, such as groceries, utilities, and so forth. You may want to set up a joint checking account—which you can do even though you're not married—to pay for household expenses that you share. Each of you must then keep a separate account to cover your personal expenditures. To make this method work, you will need to decide how much income each partner should contribute into the joint account every week or two. A 50-50 split is fair only if your incomes are about the same. If you earn one-quarter of your combined incomes, for instance, then you should contribute just one-quarter of the rent and one-quarter of the grocery and heating bills. Next, you must think about which expenses will be paid for out of this fund. This can be tricky, and sometimes you'll be splitting hairs over certain expenses. Will you pick up a restaurant tab, for instance, with the money from this account? What about a vacation? New sheets and towels? With this type of living arrangement, how you divide expenses isn't all that important. Rather, it's essential that you simply discuss these matters up front, before they become an issue and before you start feeling taken advantage of.

Property Ownership

When two unmarried people buy a house together, they can do it in two basic ways. As joint tenants with rights of survivorship, each partner shares in the ownership of the property. When you die, your share automatically passes to your surviving partner. As tenants-in-common, conversely, each of you owns a half share of the property. When you die, your share passes to whomever you've declared as the beneficiary of your estate under your will.

You might want to put down in writing how you plan to get the money out of the house if you separate. For instance, will you put the house on the market and split the proceeds according to the original contribution? Or will one of you buy the other out? How will you determine the price? Even if you're just selling the home—and not splitting up—you need to keep track of how you will divide the proceeds and how you plan to use that money.

If you're renting an apartment rather than buying a home together, find out whose name will be listed on the lease. Whoever is named on the lease is legally responsible for the rent payments. But if your name is on the lease, your partner can't simply ask you to leave when the relationship ends. As a leaseholder, you have the right to rent that property. Are you moving into your partner's apartment? Will your name be added to the lease? Some landlords won't add a name to an already existing lease.

Loans and Gifts

Many of the laws affecting spouses have to do with the transfer of property between one spouse and another. For instance, you can transfer an unlimited amount of cash or real property tax free to your spouse during your life or after your death. (See Chapter 3 for details about the unlimited marital deduction.) No such provision is extended to unmarried partners. Property transferred between you and your partner may be considered a gift—and thus subject to gift taxation.

There are special rules regarding both gifting and lending. You may gift up to $10,000 per year to each other, in cash or property, without having to file a gift tax return or pay any gift tax. Your partner (who is the recipient of the gift) doesn't have to report that gift as taxable income either. If you make a gift to your partner, though, bear in mind that the property gifted is then legally owned by your partner. You have given up all rights to the property. If either of you gifts to the other more than $10,000 per year, you will have to file a gift tax return. However, no gift tax is due until your cumulative lifetime gifts of more than $10,000 per year to nonspouses exceed $650,000. (That's the limit for 1999. Under current law, the figure will increase gradually to $1 million by the year 2006.)

For property such as a home, you can add your nonspouse partner as a joint owner with rights of survivorship. But don't treat the transfer as a gift until your death. You can accomplish this by simply documenting your intention and continuing to pay the mortgage. For the transfer to be considered a gift, you must file a gift tax return and both you and your partner must share equally in the mortgage payments. Before making any decisions about how to take title to a home with your partner, be sure to consult an attorney who specializes in such matters.

Should you decide to loan money to your partner instead of gifting it, you're entitled to charge a reasonable interest rate and to set the terms for repayment of the loan. The time frame for the loan repayment can be any period you want, and it can always be extended or renegotiated. Because this is a loan, however, you should draw up a legally binding loan agreement that clearly states the loan amount, the interest charged, and the payback period. With such an agreement, there's no room for misinterpretation by either partner in the future.

For loans under $10,000 that are not used to buy investments, it is up to you whether or not to charge interest. For loans above $10,000 (but not more than $100,000), interest is automatically imputed (that is, assumed to be charged anyway) at the government-prescribed rate for the month in which the loan was made, even if you didn't charge your partner any interest. You'll have to report interest income on your tax return—again, even if no interest was actually paid to you—if your partner earned investment income (that's interest, dividends, etc.) that year, unless he or she earned $1,000 or less. If the loans are more than $100,000, interest has to be imputed regardless of your partner's investment income.

INSURANCE AND OTHER BENEFITS

Health Insurance

In general, health insurance provided through an employer does not cover a nonspouse partner. Some companies and municipalities are changing their policies, however, so you and your partner should check with your employers to see what (and who) is covered. If you're interviewing for a new job, you may want to ask about these policies ahead of time. If your employer's health plan covers your nonspouse partner, the value of that coverage will be taxable income to you.

Life Insurance

It's important to reassess your life insurance needs when you begin your life together as a couple. Ask yourself: Could I still maintain my current lifestyle if my partner died? How would my death affect my partner's financial situation? Like a newly married pair, you may find that the basic life insurance policy offered through your employer covers your needs right now. Be sure to change your beneficiary to your partner's name: This is one detail that is often overlooked and that can lead to disaster down the road. Additional life insurance generally only becomes necessary as your joint obligations grow: for example, you have dependent children (See Chapter 5 for more information) and/or you purchase a home together. Without your partner's income, you may not be able to meet increased financial obligations and, thus, may need an additional insurance policy to fill the gap should your partner die.

You may also want to buy additional life insurance to cover the estate taxes due when one of you dies, particularly since estate taxes are generally higher if you're not married. (See the section on estate planning in this chapter for situations when this may be necessary.) You should consider the advantages and risks of putting life insurance into an irrevocable trust so that it is not taxed in either of your estates.

Retirement Plans

By federal law, a wife generally has at least a 50% interest in her husband's pension plan. That means that when the husband dies, the wife gets at least half of the pension benefit he was receiving. If he dies before retiring, she is entitled to a survivor benefit. The same law doesn't extend to nonmarried partners. While a few plans do let you name someone other than your spouse as the beneficiary, most plans don't provide survivor benefits to unmarried partners. Nor will you be eligible for survivor benefits from your partner's Social Security account.

Because of this situation, you will have to plan your retirement carefully. Some strategies you should think about (if these options are available to you):

1. Consider choosing a pension annuity with a guaranteed period of payment—even if the employee dies. That way, the surviving partner could receive payments for at least some period of time, assuming a nonspouse can be named beneficiary or is beneficiary of the estate.
2. Contribute as much as possible to your 401(k) plan, 403(b) plan, or IRA. If you are married, your spouse is automatically the beneficiary of your 401(k) or 403(b) plan. He must waive that right for you to leave the money to someone else. If you are not married, however, you can choose the beneficiary. With an IRA, you can name whomever you want as beneficiary, whether you are married or not.
3. Calculate how much additional capital each partner would need if the other partner died (and his or her pension annuity ended). Buy a life insurance policy to cover that need. It can be especially helpful if the partner who needs the proceeds, rather than the insured person, buys and holds the policy. This way the proceeds do not pass through the estate.
4. Self-insure a partial pension for the survivor. How? Each of you can build up a fund for the survivor by saving a predetermined amount from your income each month.
5. At retirement, consider taking a lump-sum distribution from your pension plan, if allowed. That way, you'll have full control over the proceeds. If your pension plan permits this (and if it makes sense, given your tax situation), you will have to decide whether to roll that distribution into an IRA or pay tax immediately (if you are eligible for favorable tax treatment allowed for lump-sum distributions). You can name a nonspouse as the beneficiary of an IRA, or, if you don't use an IRA, you can leave the assets to your partner in your will.

ESTATE PLANNING

The Importance of a Will

Whether you're married, single, divorced, or living together, a will ensures that your property is distributed to the people and/or charities you desire. If you're married, though, you have some protection even if your husband didn't have a will when he died. Upon her husband's death, a surviving wife automatically receives all or part of his estate. (See

Chapter 3 for details on spousal rights.) There is no such protection, however, for unmarried couples. If your live-in partner dies without leaving a will, you have absolutely no rights to his or her estate. Legally, you're a stranger.

Without a will, your partner's property will generally be distributed to his or her family: children (if any), parents, and/or siblings. What percentage of the estate each party will receive is determined by the laws of the state in which you live. If you have children together or if you have children from prior marriages who live with you, it's critical that both your wills specify the guardian(s) for any minor or disabled children. Otherwise, the court will decide for you. You can, of course, name each other as primary guardian if you wish, and select alternates to replace each of you should you die together.

Some unmarried partners include a provision in their wills that any bequest is only valid if the couple is still living together at death. Your will (and your partner's will) should provide for an alternate beneficiary to cover this situation, as well as an alternate executor and trustee if you have named each other to serve in those capacities now.

Trusts

If you have children from a prior marriage, you may be concerned about how much to leave to your partner and how much to your children if you should die. You generally have full discretion over your estate since it is your property. You can bequeath your assets directly to your partner and/or your children, or you can set up a trust. (See Chapter 3 for a more complete discussion of trusts.)

In this situation, you may want to consider a trust that provides income to your partner during his or her lifetime but, upon your partner's death, goes to your children. A trust can, for example, provide your partner with a lifelong income after you die. But your partner can't touch the assets. (That will prevent your partner from spending all of your money outright, or, should he or she marry or choose another partner, from bequeathing those assets to the new partner.) When your partner dies, however, the assets in the trust would pass to your children or whomever you have named as beneficiary. By setting up such a trust, you can be assured that your children (or whoever you wish) will eventually inherit your estate rather than someone your partner might choose.

A revocable living trust may also be a good idea if you want to avoid the cost and publicity of probate and if you fear that your family will question your will and the naming of your unmarried partner as beneficiary. You may want to discuss with your partner a similar arrangement for his or her assets.

Property Ownership

If property is owned by you alone, you can specify in your will to whom the property should go upon your death. If you own property with your partner, however, the beneficiary of that property will be determined by how you held title to the property while you were alive. As joint tenants with rights of survivorship, for example, both you and your partner own the property. When you die, your share automatically passes to your surviving partner—regardless of what your will says. The portion of the asset value attributable to your contributions—that includes the initial down payment and subsequent mortgage payments if the property is your home—will be included in your gross estate and possibly subject to estate tax (see the section on estate taxes in this chapter).

If you and your partner hold title to the property as tenants-in-common, however, you both own a half share of the property. When you die, your share passes to whomever you have declared as the beneficiary under your will. If that person is not a spouse, the value of the property will be included in your gross estate and will possibly be subject to estate tax (see the section on estate taxes in this chapter).

Beneficiary Designations

You can name your partner as the beneficiary of your life insurance policy, your Individual Retirement Account, and, in most cases, other defined contribution retirement plans such as a 401(k) plan, a 403(b) plan, or a Keogh plan. A beneficiary designation supersedes your will, so this is a simple way to leave assets to your partner without changing your will.

Should your living together arrangement end, remember to remove your partner's name as beneficiary if you no longer want to leave anything to him or her. That advice may seem obvious, but when I was reviewing a client's beneficiary designations, she told me the following story about a dear friend, Jill, who had recently passed away. Jill and her former partner Nancy had lived together for over 5 years. They had planned to be together forever. As the primary breadwinner, Jill feared Nancy wouldn't be able to maintain her lifestyle if she died. So she named Nancy as beneficiary of the $100,000 life insurance policy offered by her employer.

Unfortunately, the relationship ultimately dissolved. Nancy met someone else. Jill met someone else. They each went on with their lives. But Jill neglected to change that beneficiary designation. Without the formality of a legal divorce, this omission slipped between the cracks.

Several years later, Jill developed a severe heart problem. Her partner Eadie took care of her. When Jill died, however, $100,000 was paid to Nancy, who Jill hadn't spoken to in years. Eadie, who Jill would have wanted to have the insurance proceeds, didn't have a case. Legally, the money belonged to Nancy.

As the beneficiary, your partner will also have to take distributions from your IRA and all other retirement plans according to the IRS rules for nonspouses. In addition, the amounts taken out each year will be subject to income tax. Depending on the age of the deceased, a non-spouse beneficiary must, in general, take the money out within 5 years after the death of the owner of the account. However, there are some alternatives. You should consult with a financial planner or an accountant if you are in this situation.

Estate Taxes

A wife can leave as much property as she wants to her husband when she dies without incurring any estate tax, and vice versa. This is called the unlimited marital deduction. (For more details, see Chapter 3.) This rule doesn't apply to unmarried partners, however. You'll have to use other techniques to minimize your estate taxes. Everyone (married or single), for example, can leave $650,000 of property to children, friends, and/or relatives in 1999 without incurring any estate tax. This is called the unified credit equivalent. The amount will increase gradually each year, to $1 million by the year 2006.

If it seems like your estate could never be worth $650,000—and you, therefore, don't have to worry about paying estate taxes—start adding up your assets. What's the current value of your home (if you own one); your life insurance death benefit; your IRAs and 401(k) or

403(b) retirement accounts; savings and money market accounts; certificates of deposits; stocks, bonds, and other investments; collectibles and antiques; and so on? You might find that your estate is closer in value to that $650,000 limit than you think, especially when you count life insurance.

Both partners should make sure they structure their wills and trusts to make the best use of the unified credit equivalent to reduce estate taxes. It's important to understand the estate tax laws in your state. Some states have an inheritance tax on assets inherited by a nonspouse or family member.

If your life partner should die, you will have to deal with many of the same issues that a married woman does, such as handling incoming bills, making funeral arrangements, and probating the will. (See Chapters 7 and 8, which include information that can help you with these issues.)

THE COSTS—AND BENEFITS—OF THE MARITAL STATE

You and your partner may not be able to legally marry. Perhaps his divorce is not yet final, or you're a same-sex couple. You and your partner may simply not wish to marry for personal reasons. Whichever situation you're in, it is important to understand the financial consequences of your living arrangements.

Marriage does offer some financial benefits. First, you may pay less in income taxes if you are married. If only one partner has taxable income from earnings, interest, dividends, and so forth, for example, then you'll pay less income tax as a married couple than as single taxpayers. Unmarried couples might also pay more state income taxes than married couples if they live in a state with graduated tax rates that allow married couples to file either jointly or separately. Unmarried couples must file separately, which, depending on your tax situation, could mean higher taxes.

Second, as a spouse you are eligible for family health coverage under your spouse's group medical insurance plan. As an unmarried pair, you will both need your own coverage under separate plans in most cases. That can be expensive if you each have to pay for separate medical and dental coverage, or if one employer doesn't offer medical insurance and you must buy a policy on your own.

Third, if one partner doesn't work, the nonearner can't be counted as a dependent, and an unmarried partner isn't eligible for a spousal IRA.

Fourth, because you are single, each of you will have to pay to join health clubs, museums, and so on. Typically, two unmarried persons can't join under the "family" plan, which is often cheaper than two single memberships. Your entertainment/recreational costs may be higher as a result.

Finally, as an unmarried partner, you may pay more in estate, inheritance, and income taxes after your partner's death than you would if you were married. In those states that have an inheritance tax (not all do), the tax is generally higher if assets pass to a nonspouse or nonrelative (see the "Estate Planning" section in this chapter). In addition, fewer income tax planning opportunities exist for retirement plans paid to a nonspouse.

Conversely, there are some financial disadvantages to being married: namely, potentially higher income taxes. Two non-married wage earners who file separate income tax returns, for instance, usually pay lower taxes than would a married couple (see Figure 4.1). In general, the more income each partner has, the greater the income tax cost of being married. In some situations, that cost may be less than $1,000 a year, in other cases $15,000 per year or more. There are other tax deductions, such as real estate losses and IRA contributions, that may be reduced or disallowed for married couples.

For those couples who have the option to marry, it's important to review the costs and benefits with a trusted adviser before making a decision. This can be of particular importance for those who have been married or are widowed or retired.

One of my clients, Christine, wanted to marry for the second time at age 70. She had been widowed for 4 years when she met Lars, a widower. They were inseparable and happy to have found each other at this stage of their lives. Trouble was, Christine would no longer receive her husband's pension if she remarried. (Most pension benefits continue if the surviving spouse remarries. But this is not always the case, particularly with some military pensions.) Ultimately, Christine and Lars decided not to marry legally because it would cost them about $1,000 per month, which, given their budgets, they could not afford.

Of course, not all pensions have such provisions. Many provide for a surviving spouse, whatever her marital status. But you'll need to be aware of the potential problems.

FIGURE 4.1 TWO CAN'T FILE INCOME TAXES AS CHEAPLY AS ONE

John Smith and Mary Jones live together. They each earn $80,000 annually. Since they are not married, they must file as single taxpayers. Using the 1998 tax rates, their combined tax liability for the year would be $35,016.

John Smith

Gross income	$80,000
Adjusted gross income	$80,000
Less standard deduction	$ 4,250
	$75,750
Less personal exemption	$ 2,700
Taxable income	$73,050
Taxes paid	$17,508

Mary Jones

Gross income	$80,000
Adjusted gross income	$80,000
Less standard deduction	$ 4,250
	$75,750
Less personal exemption	$ 2,700
Taxable income	$73,050
Taxes paid	$17,508

John Smith and Mary Jones

Taxes paid by John Smith	$17,508
Taxes paid by Mary Jones	$17,508
Total taxes paid by both partners	$35,016

Now let's assume that John Smith and Mary Jones get married. They still earn $80,000 apiece. They've changed their tax filing status, however, to married, filing jointly. Using the 1998 tax rates, their combined tax liability for the year would be $37,151. That's $2,135 more than they paid when they filed as two single taxpayers.

John and Mary Smith

Gross income	$160,000
Adjusted gross income	$160,000
Less standard deduction	$ 7,100
	$152,900
Less personal exemption	$ 5,400
Taxable income	$147,500
Total tax paid	$ 37,151

Domestic Partner Agreements

Ever since film actors and their live-in partners began making headlines with palimony suits, unmarried couples have been questioning whether they are financially responsible for each other. Should one partner get some of the money accumulated during the relationship, for instance? If you give up your job to take care of the home, should your partner continue to provide support, even after you've split up?

A domestic partner agreement would answer such questions, and more. Basically, this agreement would serve the same function as a prenuptial agreement by spelling out in advance who pays for which expenses, how much money each partner is expected to contribute to pooled funds, and, if the couple should separate, how assets are to be divided and what if any support payments are to be made.

In addition, a domestic partner agreement should address the issue of children—either those born naturally to the partners or those adopted by the partners. In the event you and your partner separate (or one of you dies), who will be the children's guardian? Who will provide support? With whom will the children live? Even if you don't want to promise anything of an economic nature to your partner, you might want to draw up that "non-commitment" into an agreement, too. Whether these agreements are enforceable in a court of law will depend upon your state's law regarding contracts. It's crucial, therefore, that you seek competent legal counsel.

FACT

Common-Law Marriages Do Exist

Thirteen states and the District of Columbia recognize the concept of common-law marriage. (The 13 states are Alabama, Colorado, Georgia, Idaho, Iowa, Kansas, Montana, Ohio, Oklahoma, Pennsylvania, Rhode Island, South Carolina, and Texas.) In these states, a man and woman will be considered a married couple *under common law* if they have lived together as husband and wife for a certain number of years. Even in these states, however, common law marriage applies only to heterosexual couples.

LOOKING AHEAD:
What You Should Be Doing Right Now

1. Decide how you're going to divide expenses.
2. Make an inventory of items each partner brings to the relationship. Even small items could be of issue at some later date.
3. Decide how you're going to handle ownership of property.
4. Write a will. Will you leave your assets in trust for your children?
5. Review your insurance policies. Will you be able to maintain your current lifestyle if your partner dies? If not, you may want to suggest a bigger life insurance policy.
6. Plan for retirement. Unlike a married partner, you're not automatically eligible for part of your partner's pension plan. Do you have sufficient funds elsewhere?
7. Consider the potential costs of not being married.
8. Familiarize yourself with the common-law marriage rules of your state.
9. Consider drawing up a domestic partner arrangement. Like a prenuptial agreement, this could help you define not only who gets what if you split up but how your lives together will be conducted from a financial standpoint.

THE SANDWICH GENERATION: CARING FOR YOUR CHILDREN AND YOUR ELDERLY PARENTS

Your children are young and need your constant care. Or perhaps they're in their 20s but still rely on you for emotional and financial support. Your parents, on the other hand, are getting older and frailer. You worry about them. Perhaps you're already responsible for their daily care.

And then there's you, sandwiched between these two generations with their numerous demands on your time, energy, and financial resources. Unfortunately, there is a good chance that the problems and concerns of raising your children and caring for your elderly parents simultaneously will fall to a great extent on your shoulders. Caregiving has traditionally been considered women's work, and, for the most part, it still is.

Caring for Your Children

Like most parents, you probably feel you would do anything for your children. Stay up all night if they're sick. Play 10 games of Candyland—in a row. Even stand in line at the store for 3 hours to get the year's hottest toy. But have you done all you can to prepare for their future? Have you written a will, chosen a guardian, bought enough life insurance, and started putting money aside for college tuition? These are the financial issues that will most likely concern you at this point in your life.

Living on One Income or Two

The decision of whether or not to work while your children are young is a tough one that all couples must make. For some, this decision is made solely for economic reasons: Both parents must work in order to pay the bills. In other cases, it has little to do with the family's financial situation. Perhaps you have a job that is immensely satisfying. Perhaps you have invested great time and effort to advance your career and you don't want to stop in midstream. Or perhaps you feel that staying at home with children all day long goes against your nature. You envision yourself as bored, frustrated, and isolated from all the excitement "out there."

Most families, however, fall somewhere between these two extremes. Two incomes mean more money to spend and save. But daily life is more hectic and stressful, and you spend less time with your children. A one-income family is simpler because one parent devotes his or her time to the children. But you have less money to spend and save, and that could put some strain on your budget and your future financial security. When does it make sense for both spouses to work? Does a dual income really pay off?

The answer isn't clear. The spending habits of families vary so widely, depending upon everything from the type of child care they use to the kind of lifestyle they lead, that it's almost impossible to generalize about how lucrative a second income actually is. But before you decide to keep your job—or call it quits—consider the following:

Much of That Second Salary May Be Eaten Up by Taxes. It is easy to forget how much of your income goes to Uncle Sam. That's especially true if one spouse is self-employed and must pay the full self-employment tax. You pay 7.65% on the first $68,400 of wages in 1998 if you're an employee; the other 7.65% is paid by your company. If you are self-employed, however, you pay the full 15.3% yourself (although you do get a deduction for half the tax you pay). Depending upon your income, a second income could also push the family into a higher income tax bracket; in any case, taxes on the second income will be imposed at your highest marginal rate.

Here's how the income tax system works: You pay a certain percentage of tax based on your overall taxable income (that's your income after deductions and personal exemptions) and your filing status (i.e., married, filing jointly or single, head of household). There are currently five tax brackets ranging from 15% to 39.6%. If you are in the 28% tax bracket, you pay 15% on your taxable income up to a certain level that varies based on your filing status. You then pay 28% on your taxable income over that threshold, and so on. Your average tax on your taxable income will fall somewhere between 15% and 28%, but you'll pay 28% on your last dollar (plus the FICA tax).

Much of That Second Salary May Be Eaten Up by Expenses. It costs money to have a job. You need work-related attire and money for commuting, lunch, and childcare. As a full-time worker, you will probably have less time for chores, so you may spend additional money on cleaning services and prepared foods or eating out.

Continuing to Earn a Salary Means You're Investing in Your Future Earnings Potential. You may not see much of your paycheck now, but if you stay in the workforce, you will be investing in your future. At some point you'll get a raise or a promotion. Your income stream will grow progressively. Women who drop out of paid employment, conversely, usually cannot reenter at the same level at which they left. If you stay out long enough, your earning power may be severely diminished. Or you may have to incur the time and expense to get retrained to catch up with changes in the workplace or go back to school to study for an entirely different career.

Some Work-Related Expenses Will Decrease over Time. Child care costs, typically the biggest expense for working mothers, don't last forever. Once your child goes to school, for example, child care costs will lessen and eventually go away. Work attire is expensive at first but as you build a wardrobe of work clothes, annual costs go down.

Continuing to Earn a Salary Lets You Continue to Build Up Your Own Retirement Fund. If your employer offers a 401(k) or 403(b) plan at work, that could be a hidden benefit of remaining in the workforce. In the short term, your 401(k) or 403(b) contributions give you a tax break. Because you put pre-tax dollars into these plans, you save money in federal and state income taxes now. In addition, the money you put into the account grows tax deferred. The more you put in, the larger your retirement fund will be. If your employer matches all or part of your contribution, you are getting additional funds that you wouldn't get if you quit your job. Compared to men as a whole, women as a group have not focused as much on these long-term planning issues. As a result, they may face more financial difficulties as they age and retire. (See Chapter 10 for more information about women and retirement.)

Without a Salary, You May Be Putting Yourself at Risk. Divorce and widowhood are facts of life. As a wife who does not work outside the home, you could be forced suddenly to support your children. Could you quickly get a satisfactory job again? Would it pay enough to meet your financial obligations? Most women who get divorced, especially those who have been out of the workplace for years, experience a significant drop in their standard of living.

A Case Study: The Cost of Working

Diana stopped working outside the home after the birth of her first child. She devoted her time to raising her family and supporting her husband's career as an executive at a large corporation.

That was 20 years ago. As Diana's children grew older—and became independent—she began thinking about a new career for herself. She had often been complimented on her decorating abilities, so she began talking about becoming an interior decorator. She hoped to earn $50,000 per year.

Diana knew that she would have some expenses setting up her business, and, of course, she would have to pay income taxes on her earnings. However, Bob's $500,000 salary meant that they were in the top income tax bracket. Including state tax, 47% of each additional dollar of the couple's combined income would go to taxes. In addition, because she would be self-employed, Diana would have to pay both halves of the 15.3% FICA tax. At first glance, the added FICA burden didn't seem so bad. Most of it (12.4%) goes to Social Security. But in Diana's case, that doesn't give her anything she doesn't already have. When she reaches age 62, Diana is eligible to receive 50% of her husband's Social Security benefit. That's true whether or not she contributes something to Social Security through her own employment. Diana will probably never earn enough to qualify to receive a benefit (from her own earnings) that is higher than 50% of Bob's benefit. Ultimately, any FICA tax that Diana pays will provide her with no benefits at all. Diana has to consider if working for pay is actually worth it!

Estate Planning

Estate planning is crucial as a means of providing for your family over the long term. Whether you're a working mother who's also the family breadwinner or a stay-at-home mother, you should understand what your estate includes, what taxes (if any) will be borne by your estate, and what arrangements need to be made for your children. Failure to talk about—and thus plan for—your death won't spare your loved ones. On the contrary, they will have less control (and more legal hassles to deal with). Think of your children without you around to care for their needs and support them with love. Keep that idea in mind as you consider the four estate planning issues that are especially crucial to women with children:

- The importance of a will
- The importance of trusts
- The usefulness of a testamentary trust (a trust created in your will during your lifetime but funded at death)
- The importance of custodial accounts

The Importance of a Will. As a parent, you need a will—even if you have minimal assets. If you and your spouse die intestate (without a will), any assets that you don't own as joint tenants with rights of survivorship or that don't have a beneficiary designation will be divided by a judge in probate court according to the laws of your state. That fact may not mean all that much to you. Without a will, the house, the car, and the bank accounts will likely pass to your spouse and kids, which may be precisely the distribution you had in mind anyway. But a will also designates your child's guardian and gives you the ability to establish trusts, to minimize taxes, to manage your assets, and to make distributions in keeping with your wishes. Without a will, a judge will decide—in the event both you and your husband die—who is best suited to raise your children. And, unless you clarify your wishes about guardianship in your will, there's no guarantee that the judge will appoint the guardian you would have selected to care for your children and manage the money you have set aside for them.

The guardian of the child is responsible for your child's day-to-day care following your death. Most parents choose a guardian who shares their values and lifestyle, such as a brother, sister, or a parent. If you're divorced, guardianship generally falls to your ex-spouse, assuming he wants to raise the children and is capable of doing so.

If you select a guardian who is warm and loving—but whose financial management skills are limited—it's wise to place the assets in trust or appoint another person, known as the *guardian of the estate,* to manage your child's financial affairs. (This is especially important if the child will receive a large inheritance.) State laws require the guardian of the estate to use the money and other assets bequeathed to the child for the child's support, maintenance, and education. A periodic accounting is required by the court to ensure that the money is being used solely for the child's needs.

A *trustee,* on the other hand, is a person or an institution such as a bank, appointed by you in your will to manage the assets in a specific trust. The trustee manages the trust property and must spend it according to the instructions written in your will. The trust is a separate taxable entity and the trustee is responsible for filing all required state and federal income tax returns for the trust and for paying the taxes.

Your E&Y Planner Says:

Whom should you appoint as guardian of your child? Clients sometimes lament that this particular decision is just too hard. But, tough as this task may be, you must do it—the sooner the better.

Should you and your husband die tomorrow without naming a guardian, a judge will do his or her best to pick a guardian, based on testimony from your friends and relatives who are willing to care for your child. But it is quite possible that your children may be left with someone you would not have chosen as their guardian. As trite as it sounds, mother (and father) really do know best in this situation. Also, think of a second choice for guardian and trustee, in case your first choice declines or dies.

In addition, depending upon the guardian you pick, you may have to make some additional provisions in your will for the guardian (in the event you and your husband both die). For example, if your sister or brother, who has a modest income, is designated as the children's guardian, you may want to give her or him some share of your estate (in addition to what you would have left her or him otherwise). You don't want raising your children to create a financial hardship for the guardian, and you want your children to continue to live the lifestyle that you have established for them.

Peter and Jennifer, for instance, worried about what would happen to their children if they died at the same time. To protect their children should this happen, their wills state that Jennifer's brother James would raise the children. If James dies, Peter's brother Bill would take over as guardian.

James currently lives in a one-bedroom apartment. So Jennifer and Peter set up a trust in his name. The proceeds from the trust could be used to purchase a larger home. This would allow the children to move in with their uncle without creating a financial hardship for him.

The Usefulness of a Testamentary Letter. In addition to your will, you should consider writing a testamentary letter. While your will may provide instructions for the distribution of your larger assets, such as your home, your car, and your bank accounts, a testamentary letter designates who gets your smaller possessions, such as china, family photographs, jewelry, mementos, and so forth. If this document is handwritten and referenced in your will, it is generally legally binding and can save many an argument over material possessions among family members. More important, it will make clear to your parents and siblings exactly what you wish your children to have. This way your children will get the items you have always had in mind for them. Make sure the letter is kept in an easy-to-find place—perhaps with your attorney—and is up to date.

The Importance of Trusts and Custodial Accounts. Minor children can't legally own much property without adult supervision—and for good reason. Unfortunately, leaving too much money directly to children or young adults can have detrimental rather than happy consequences. The ready availability of money may wither or end the incentive to work, and children may lose the joy and sense of reward that come from individual accomplishment. Some parents do not have the confidence in the ability of their children to prudently manage significant sums of money. They are concerned that the inheritance might be dissipated if not properly supervised. To transfer money to your children, you can either set up a trust or a custodial account.

Custodial Accounts. Under the Uniform Gifts (or Transfers) to Minors Act (UGMA), you can shift ownership of assets such as securities to your minor child. A custodian (you, your spouse, or a third party) manages the account until your child reaches adulthood. (Children reach the age of majority between 18 and 21, depending upon the rules of the state in which you live.)

The advantages are clear. Income earned on the account during the custodial period is taxable to the minor, subject to kiddie tax provisions (see the box later in this section). In addition, if you are not the custodian, you remove the assets—and all future growth of those assets—from your estate, thereby reducing the size of your estate and your subsequent estate tax liability. Finally, through a planned program, you may be able to gift your assets to your kids without incurring any gift tax (see the box later in this chapter).

The downside of custodial accounts: Your gifts are irrevocable. You can't change your mind and take the money back—even if you need it a few years later to pay unexpected medical bills or to fund a business venture. Typically, you can't use the income from a custodial account to pay for living expenses and support of your child while he or she is your dependent, either. (Otherwise, the income would be taxable to you, which defeats one of the primary purposes of establishing the account in the first place.) In addition, you can't control how your child uses the funds once he or she comes of age. That means that if you put money for college into an UGMA account and your child decides to spend it all on a trip around the world instead of four years of college, there's legally nothing you can do about it.

Annual Gift Tax Exclusion

You may give up to $10,000 every year to each of your children (or to any other person) without incurring any gift tax. If your husband joins in making the gift, you may (as a couple) give $20,000 to each child annually without any gift tax liability. This is called the *annual gift tax exclusion*. All gifts that fall within the exclusion limits are protected from federal and gift estate taxes, making regular use of the annual gift tax exclusion one of the easiest ways to reduce the size of your taxable estate and provide a nest egg for your children's future. In order to qualify, the recipient needs to have immediate access to the gift or it must be placed in a special type of trust known as a minor's trust. If the recipient won't need it while he or she is young, the gifts you give over the years could be your child's down payment on his or her first home. Wouldn't you have liked that help when you were first starting out? Even a couple of hundred dollars a year now could mean a big difference in the future.

Kiddie Tax

The tax laws used to be simpler—at least for kids. Since 1987, however, children must now frequently file tax returns on income earned from an investment (unearned income) in their name. Known as the kiddie tax, this new tax is meant to discourage parents from sheltering investment income in their child's name. Here's how it works: Generally, your child's first $700 (in 1998) in unearned income is tax free. The second $700 (in 1998) is taxed at 15%, the lowest bracket for federal income tax. After that, if a child is under age 14, any additional unearned income is taxed at the rate you, the parent, would pay on this income. When your child turns 14, however, he or she pays the tax based on his or her own rates, which is probably a lower amount.

Trusts. As a parent, you must decide not only how much money your children will inherit from your estate but when they will receive that inheritance. You can give your children complete access to all funds when they reach the age of majority (between 18 or 21 years of age, depending upon the state in which you live), or you can create a trust so that they don't get all of the money at once.

Trusts allow a good deal of flexibility. For example, you can instruct the trustee to disburse funds at different intervals: for example, one-third of the inheritance at age 25, another third at age 30, and the remainder at age 35. Sequenced distributions such as these may give your children an opportunity to learn to manage money. At the very least, you will not have to worry that your children might spend their entire nest egg at once.

You can set up one trust for all of your children. Frequently, once the youngest reaches age 25, the trust dissolves and each child gets an equal share.

A CASE STUDY: WHEN YOUR CHILDREN CAN'T LEAVE HOME

"I've heard about the sandwich generation," Jessie said. "I'm a triple-decker."

Jessie, age 75, came from a closely-knit multigenerational family. Her father, Caesar, 97, still lived with Jessie and her husband, John, 85. John had been healthy until a few months ago when he was diagnosed with cancer. The prognosis wasn't good. The couple's youngest child, Charlie, also lived with them. Charlie, 35, had Down's syndrome. Though he worked hard on his paper route and helped his brothers in their landscaping business, he would never be able to live on his own.

Jessie wasn't getting any younger. She needed to make plans for herself and the rest of the family. Jessie frequently took care of her grandchildren while her sons and daughters were working. Who would care for them when she couldn't?

That's when Jessie came to see me. We talked about her situation. Jessie could reasonably expect to outlive Caesar and John. Caesar was well provided for, but Jessie had to make sure that John was taken care of should she die first. She included John as a beneficiary in her will, but added a clause that excluded him if he predeceased her. That's a standard clause in a will, but alarmingly, Jessie's previous will did not include such a clause.

Next she needed to name a guardian for Charlie. Jessie wanted to name her daughter Janet but was concerned because Janet wasn't a good money manager. I suggested that she leave the money to Charlie in trust, with several of the other children as trustees. That way Charlie would have the benefit of Janet's love and his other siblings' financial savvy.

Finally, we talked about the grandchildren. I explained the generation-skipping trust to Jessie. It's designed to benefit grandchildren. In such a setup, the trust beneficiaries—generally your grandchildren—must be at least two generations your juniors. You can, however, stipulate in the trust document that your own children may receive the trust income and even tap its principal to pay for virtually anything including housing, health care for the entire family, and the grandchildren's college education. In this case, Jessie's grandchildren are the beneficiaries of the generation-skipping trust. But their parents (Jessie's children) are entitled to the trust income—and have control over the principal. When Jessie's children die, the assets remaining in the trust will go to the grandchildren without ever being diminished by taxes imposed on her children's estate.

Insuring Your Family's Well-Being

Insurance is a necessary part of protecting your family's financial future. It's something you buy but hope you will never have to use. Some people don't buy enough insurance and think that by avoiding the issue they can wish all of their worries away. But that simply doesn't work. No one ever expects to die young. No one ever expects to be disabled. Yet bad things sometimes happen to us and those we love. You can keep all the financial risk that goes along with the unexpected or you can shift a lot of that financial risk by buying insurance. You pay now to avoid a financial disaster in the future.

If you are a wife and mother, it's crucial that you have enough insurance coverage. The proper amount of life insurance will protect your husband and children should you die prematurely. The proper amount of disability insurance will protect you and your family should you have an accident and be unable to return to work. When you buy an insurance policy, what you are ultimately buying is some peace of mind that your family will be protected should tragedy strike. And that is a protection no family should be without.

Life Insurance. People buy life insurance so that their family's needs will be met if the breadwinner dies, or to provide for child care if the primary caregiver dies. As a parent, you need life insurance when your children are young and dependent upon you for their food, shelter, and education. How much life insurance will you need exactly? Unfortunately, there isn't one answer. Every family's needs are different.

To figure out how much insurance you need, you must carefully examine your family's expenses and its sources of income. How much income will your family need after you die to meet its expenses? How long should that income continue? Typically, you don't insure your lifetime earnings, just the cost of raising your children and putting them through college. Most parents want insurance to do the following:

- Fund the kids' college educations
- Provide income for your spouse so that he can provide care for the kids
- Pay funeral expenses

In the past, the male breadwinner was typically the only parent insured. But today so many mothers work outside the home that if both parents earn a paycheck, both should be insured. Even if you are a stay-at-home mom, insuring yourself makes a lot of sense. If you do all the cooking, cleaning, and child care, your husband would have to pay someone to perform those services if you died. Could he meet those expenses out of the monthly cash flow? If not, you need an insurance policy. If this is your circumstance, consider at least a small policy that will cover these expenses until your children are independent.

Children generally don't need to be insured. They don't provide any income that needs to be replaced, and statistically, it's unlikely that they will die before you. Still, some people do buy cash-value life insurance policies on their children and use the cash value as an investment. You can borrow against the policy (to some extent), for example, to pay for college tuition.

Other parents buy life insurance policies for their children as protection in case a child develops a debilitating illness and dies. The death benefit would help the family pay for extensive medical bills and funeral costs. Similarly, some parents buy insurance for children because it's inexpensive. This ground floor coverage could last the child throughout adulthood. It could also prove especially important if the child has difficulty obtaining insurance coverage later on in life due to an illness. However, you should not buy life insurance for your child until you and your husband (the child's parents) are adequately insured.

During the early years of parenthood, most couples typically cover their insurance needs with term insurance. Term insurance is the simplest kind of insurance you can buy, and generally the least expensive. You pay premiums for a set term. If you die during that time, the insurance company pays a death benefit to your beneficiary (your husband or the kids). Unlike cash-value insurance, however, term products have no savings or investment features. You can't borrow against this policy or surrender it for some cash because there is no cash buildup. Still, term policies are often the best insurance product for young couples because they offer the most coverage for the least amount of money.

There are two kinds of term insurance: annually renewable term and level premium term. With annually renewable term insurance, your premium goes up every year. Why? Statistically, you're more likely to die as you get older. Level premium term insurance costs more per year initially than the annually renewable kind, but the premiums stay level for a period of 5, 10, 15, or even 20 years. And you don't have to go through the process of renewing your policy each year. This could also be a benefit should you become ill. With annual renewal, you might not be able to keep your life insurance if you are diagnosed with a terminal illness.

If your discretionary income permits, you should consider investing in at least some cash-value insurance. Cash-value policies, which initially cost more than term policies, offer traditional life insurance protection—plus a variety of savings, investment, and payment options. Your premium buys you some life insurance; the remainder is put into an account where it grows on a tax-deferred basis. You'll receive the surrender value of the policy if you decide in the future that you no longer want it. The difference between the amount you receive and the total amount you paid in premiums is subject to tax if surrendered before death.

There are three basic types of cash-value policies: whole life, universal life, and variable life. Whole life, the traditional cash-value insurance product, is designed to cover you for your whole life. You pay a fixed premium for the life of the policy. Universal life, by contrast, is more flexible. It allows you (within certain limits) to determine your own premium. The third type, variable life, differs from the other two products because it allows you to select how the cash value is invested from among certain investment choices.

> ### Your E&Y Planner Says:
>
> Many people get life insurance coverage through their jobs. But it's rarely enough, especially if you are the mother of young children. Employers typically offer a standard policy to everyone; they don't sit down and actually calculate how much life insurance each employee needs. It's your responsibility to figure out how much coverage you need, and, if necessary, to buy additional policies from an insurance agent. (See Chapter 11 for information on choosing an insurance agent.)
>
> Some employers offer an option to buy more insurance. This is usually at a competitive rate. It may be cost effective for you to cover as much of your insurance needs as possible this way. Keep in mind, however, that if you leave your job, your insurance coverage may leave, too. Check to see if your policy is portable.

Disability Insurance. If you're in your 30s or 40s, you have a much greater chance of being disabled than dying. A 35-year-old has about a 1 in 3 chance of becoming disabled for at least 6 months before reaching age 65 (see Figure 5.1). The question you need to ask yourself, then, is: "What would happen to my family finances if I had a heart attack and couldn't work?" Many employers offer long-term disability coverage. If yours does not, you should purchase it from a licensed insurance agent.

As a general rule, insurers limit the disability coverage you can purchase to 60% of your gross income. The cost of an individual policy

Age	Number per 1,000 Still Disabled after 90 Days	Number per 1,000 Dying at a Given Age	Chance of Disability Compared with Chance of Death
32	7.78	2.25	3.34 to 1
42	12.57	4.17	3.01 to 1
52	22.72	9.96	2.28 to 1

FIGURE 5.1 YOU HAVE A GREATER CHANCE OF BECOMING DISABLED THAN OF DYING IN A GIVEN YEAR

varies, depending upon your age, your sex, your occupation, and the policy's features, such as definition of disability, inflation protection, residual benefits, and the waiting period until benefits start. Older people pay more than younger people, for example. Workers in high-risk occupations pay more than those in low-risk occupations. (For instance, a police officer is more likely to be shot than a file clerk.)

When purchasing an individual policy, you will have to make a decision pertaining to the following aspects of disability coverage:

- *Definition of disability.* Some policies stipulate that you are disabled if you can't continue your usual work. Other polices claim you're disabled only if you can't work at all. The more liberal the definition, the higher the cost of the policy.
- *Residual benefits.* Without a residual benefits clause, your benefits would cease if you went back to work part time after becoming disabled.
- *Waiting period.* How long must you wait before disability benefits begin? Typical waiting periods are 30, 60, 90, 120, and 180 days. The longer the wait, the lower the premiums.
- *Benefit period.* Short-term policies that pay benefits for up to 2 years cost less than long-term policies that pay benefits until age 65 if you become permanently disabled.
- *Renewability and noncancelability.* A guaranteed renewable, noncancelable policy means that the insurer can't cancel your policy if you continue to pay the premiums. Most issuers will cancel the policy, though, once you reach the age at which you can start collecting Social Security benefits.

- *Cost-of-living escalator.* This feature covers for inflation. The younger you are, the more valuable this feature is.
- *Waiver of premium.* This means that if you become disabled, you won't have to pay any premiums during the period of disability.

FACT

Stay-at-Home Mothers Have No Disability Coverage

And you can't buy it either. Even though you would probably have to pay someone to fill your shoes while you were recuperating from a heart attack, you can't buy a disability policy to protect yourself. Why? Technically, you have no earnings to replace because you're not actually employed. You need to set up an emergency fund to cover this possibility.

Health Insurance. Obtaining sufficient health insurance is as important as having enough life and disability insurance. You probably receive your health coverage through your employer and/or your husband's employer. (See Chapter 1 for the options generally available.) If you're self-employed, you will have to buy your own policy. Group policies, which are generally less expensive, may be available to you through a professional or trade association.

If you stop working during the early years of parenthood to stay at home with your children, you'll have to rely solely upon your husband's health coverage, assuming of course that his employer provides such coverage. That may limit your options because you will now have only one plan to choose from. But, if both you and your husband continue to work and receive health coverage, you may be able to get virtually all of your health care costs covered by insurance. You should decide on one plan as the primary insurer, based on the coverage, deductibles, and co-insurance requirements.

Funding a College Education

Most parents worry about how they are going to fund their child's college education. You want to send your child to a school that best meets his or her needs—but you don't want to completely exhaust your savings to do it.

College tuition rises every year, often 2 to 3 percentage points higher than the rate of inflation. When your son (who is now 6 years old) is ready for college in the year 2010, it's estimated that the annual cost of his college education will be $60,341 at an Ivy League school, $41,484 at an out-of-state university, and $22,628 at a state university. Those numbers can discourage even the most disciplined savers.

Your best bet is to start your child's college fund as early as possible, and to put money regularly into that account. That's easier said than done, of course. In the early years of your child's life, you may find that you don't have much extra to put aside as savings. But, again, don't be discouraged. Once your child marches off to kindergarten, you will probably find yourself with a bit more cash on hand. Expenses such as frequent doctor visits and child care, which can take a substantial bite out of your budget, are reduced during the grade school years. Also, you may be returning to paid employment at this point after staying at home, unpaid, with the children for a number of years. Earmark a percentage of your total income for building a college fund.

What types of savings or investment accounts are appropriate for education funding? First, you must consider your time horizon: When do you need the money? In general, if college costs are still a long way off—more than 7 years in the future, for instance—you can put your money in any investment that meets your needs, such as stocks, bonds, or mutual funds that combine both stocks and bonds. But it's often advisable, since you have such a long time horizon, to invest at least two-thirds of your education fund in stocks or stock mutual funds. The reasoning: Stocks have consistently delivered better returns over time than bonds or cash investments. In the short term, however, stocks are much riskier investments. So, if you invest in stocks today, you'll need to change your investment to bonds or cash in the future as the college tuition payment date approaches.

Another often recommended investment for long-term savings is a dedicated bond. That is, you purchase a bond that matures at the exact point in time when you need the money. This can be an effective and simple strategy. You might buy a bond, for instance, that will mature just before your child's freshman year of college begins. (Actually you'll want the bond to mature in July or August, when you must write that first tuition check.) Zero-coupon bonds are a popular choice because these bonds reinvest their interest automatically (which means you don't have to reinvest interest income on a semiannual basis). Of course, buying bonds for college funding means you need cash up front for the initial purchase, which is not always possible. But, you could use a windfall such as a bonus, inheritance, or gift from the child's grandparents to get started.

If college costs are starting in the intermediate term—about 3 to 7 years—you risk being unable to meet them if you invest in stocks and stock mutual funds. You should put no more than 50% of your college savings into these types of investments. The remaining funds should be put into dedicated bonds or Series EE bonds. If college costs are due in the short term—less than 3 years—you should probably invest entirely in less risky investments, such as federally insured certificates of deposit and money market accounts. Series EE bonds may still make sense if you will receive the added benefit of not having to pay tax on the investment income.

You may also consider an Education IRA. You can make contributions of up to $500 per child per year to an Education IRA as long as you meet certain income requirements. While your contributions are not tax deductible, the earnings are free from income tax if they are used for educational purposes.

The government can also help offset the cost of tuition with two education tax credits: the HOPE Scholarship Credit and the Lifetime Learning Credit. You may elect only one of these two tax credits or a withdrawal from a tax-free Education IRA for each eligible student in each taxable year.

The HOPE Scholarship Credit is worth up to $1,500 (100% of the first $1,000 and 50% of the second $1,000) per year for each student attending college. The credit can only be applied for the first two years of education, and the student must attend school at least half time. Beginning in 2002, the amount of the HOPE Scholarship Credit will be adjusted for inflation.

The Lifetime Learning Credit is worth up to 20% of tuition and fees for undergraduate and graduate school education. Unlike the HOPE Scholarship Credit, a taxpayer may claim the Lifetime Learning Credit for an unlimited number of tax years. The maximum credit per taxpayer return, regardless of the number of students in college, is $1,000 for $5,000 of qualified education expenses. In the year 2003, the maximum credit increases to $2,000 for $10,000 of qualified education expenses.

Sources of Education Funding

Like most parents, you probably won't fund the entire cost of your child's college education. Instead, you will use some combination of the following:

- *Current earnings.* You may have more discretionary income now that your children are older, especially if you are working full time.
- *Savings.* Start saving as soon as possible. Gradually switch from risky investments to safer accounts as your time horizon shortens.
- *Federal and state grants.* This money is given to students who meet certain financial requirements.
- *Scholarships.* This money is awarded by schools and other entities (e.g., religious groups and foundations) to students who are outstanding in academics, the arts, or athletics.
- *Work-study.* In these programs, the student pays for a portion of his or her tuition by working at a part-time job.

Even the most rigorous savings and investment program, however, may leave you short on college funds. As a result, you may have to consider borrowing money to meet your child's tuition bills. You have several alternatives from which to choose.

Home Equity Loans. If you own a home, you may be able to borrow against the equity in your house to pay for college. (In most cases, you can borrow up to 80% of your home's equity.) The advantage is that interest on home equity loans up to $100,000 is tax deductible.

Loans against Retirement Plans. If you have a 401(k) or some other qualified retirement plan, you can often borrow up to 50% of your account's assets up to $50,000. Generally, the loan must be repaid with interest over 5 years. (The repayment period is longer for home mortgages.) The advantage: The interest is typically paid back to your own account. The disadvantage: It hurts your long-term value for retirement and you pay double tax on the interest since you cannot get a tax deduction for the interest but you will pay tax on the interest earnings when the 401(k) is cashed out. You are also replacing pre-tax contributions with after-tax money.

Borrowing against Cash-Value Life Insurance. You can borrow from the cash surrender value of most life insurance policies without incurring any tax on the amount received. Interest rates will vary, depending on the age and type of policy.

Student Loans. Stafford loans allow college freshmen to borrow up to $2,625 for the first year of college and $3,500 for the second year. Juniors and seniors can borrow up to $5,500 annually. Stafford loans are available in subsidized and unsubsidized versions. The Student Loan Marketing Association (Sallie Mae) offers PLUS loans to parents. Perkins loans are granted to lower-income students. The Educational Resources Institute (TERI) Loans are available through local designated banks. Loan amounts start at $2,000 per year, but can run as high as the total cost of the tuition.

> ### Your E&Y Planner Says:
>
> Retirement savings versus the college fund? If you have a limited amount of money to save—and you're wondering if you should be saving for your child's college tuition or your own retirement— think of yourself first. You must have enough money to retire. That's your first goal. You can't do everything for your kids. You could wind up with insufficient funds in your old age, and your kids may not be able to help you or be as generous with their money.
>
> In addition, retirement savings are not currently included as assets in most financial aid calculations. Thus, if you put most of your assets in retirement savings, your child may have a better chance of qualifying for financial aid.

Caring for Your Aging Parents

As your parents get on in years, you may find that they are relying on you more and more. What starts merely as lending a hand with the weekly grocery shopping or helping them sort through their mail and pay their bills may ultimately turn into complete responsibility for their financial and physical well-being. It may almost seem as though you have switched roles: Your parents are now completely dependent upon you for guidance and support, much as you were on them when you were a young child.

The issues that will most likely concern you and your aging parents are health and money management matters.

Health Care Issues

If your parents are age 65 or older, and are eligible for Social Security, they may believe that Medicare will take care of any health care costs. Although Medicare Parts A and B will probably cover a significant portion of their medical needs, Medicare simply doesn't cover everything. For example, Medicare does not pay for long-term custodial care in a nursing home after the first 100 days.

It's quite possible, of course, that your parents may need such specialized care someday, but be unable to afford it. That means you will have to either help your parents pay those bills or care for them yourself. In planning for the future, then, you may wish to suggest that your parents purchase a Medigap policy or a Medicare HMO to supplement their Medicare benefits. Both are designed to cover the gaps in traditional Medicare coverage. (For a full discussion of Medicare benefits and Medigap policies, see Chapter 10.) You may also want to consider helping them purchase a long-term care insurance policy or purchasing it for them.

The Cost of Long-Term Care. Many women worry that their parents will require long-term care in a nursing home or similar convalescent facility. And rightly so. This type of nursing care is very expensive. Costs vary across the country and are typically higher in major metropolitan areas (see Figure 5.2). Yet neither health insurance nor Medicare covers the cost.

Nursing home fees must be paid either with cash, by Medicaid, or through long-term care insurance (see the section on long-term care insurance in this chapter). If your parents do not have substantial assets or income, Medicaid may cover long-term care costs. But your parents will only qualify after they've used up almost all their com-

---

FIGURE 5.2   AVERAGE ELDER CARE COSTS

Type of Care	Typical Cost
Nursing home	$36,000–$72,000 per year
Continuing care retirement community	$2,000 per month (after initial fee)
Assisted living	$1,000–$2,000 per month
Adult day care	$40–$70 per day
Registered nurse	$30–$50 per hour
Home care worker	$10–$14 per hour

Sources: *Money, The Inside Guide to America's Nursing Homes, The Detroit News, Forbes, Consumer Digest.*

---

bined savings and they will only be able to go to facilities that accept Medicaid. A spouse has a legal obligation to pay for a patient's long-term care. A child does not.

Medicaid rules vary by state, but all states currently set limits on how much a person can own before Medicaid will kick in. For instance, a patient typically can't hold more than $3,000 in assets; the patient's spouse can hold assets ranging from $16,000 to $80,000; all but a few dollars of the patient's income must be used to offset nursing home costs; and the spouse's income can't exceed $2,000 per month. Assets that Medicaid won't touch include the patient's or spouse's home and car. Even if these assets are protected, and they qualify for Medicaid, you may find yourself having to assist your parents financially by buying their necessities.

Like other people struggling to meet these high costs, your parents might prefer to give away their assets rather than spend them on a nursing home. This is a complex issue, however. It's illegal for an advisor to tell your parents to give away assets so that they will be eligible for Medicaid, for instance. And even if your parents do manage to give away most of their assets, they can't apply for Medicaid benefits right away. They must wait 3 years after making an outright gift of assets, 5 years if they transferred assets to a trust. In addition, giving away assets always leaves an older person financially vulnerable—whether he or she ultimately needs long-term nursing care or not.

FACT **An Estimated 43% of Current Senior Citizens Will Spend Time in a Nursing Home**

If possible, don't wait until a crisis arises to address the issue of long-term care. Help your parents examine the options ahead of time. Consider possible alternatives to a nursing home, such as in-home care, an assisted living facility, or adult day care.

Long-Term Care Insurance. Long-term care insurance is expensive, but it will pay for nursing home, convalescent facility, or in-home care when it's needed. If your parents never need such care, the money invested in the policy cannot be recouped. But if your parents do need such care, the benefits will likely outweigh the costs of the insurance. It will help them avoid losing all their assets, and will help you avoid having to assist them financially.

Typically, a person buys long-term care insurance to protect his or her assets. If your parents' assets (excluding their home and car) are worth less than $50,000, long-term care insurance is probably not worth its cost. But if your parents' assets are somewhat substantial—and they want to remain financially independent and/or pass an inheritance to you or your children—a long-term care policy may make sense.

Coverage can vary widely from policy to policy. It's important that you understand what is covered and what is not. Make sure the insurance doesn't duplicate the skilled nursing coverage provided by Medicaid, a Medigap policy, a managed care plan, or some other supplementary coverage your parents have. Other important features to evaluate before purchasing a long-term care policy include the following:

The Daily Benefit. How much will the policy pay per day? (Most pay anywhere from $50 to $250 per day.) Is that amount sufficient to cover the cost of nursing home or in-home care where your parents live?

The Waiting Period. Most insurance plans will start paying after your parent has been in a facility for a specified period of time, such as 60 or 100 days. Consider selecting a longer waiting period to reduce the premium.

The Services Covered. Some policies cover nursing homes only. Those policies that offer in-home coverage generally cost more.

Exclusions. Not all medical care is covered. For instance, the care needed for certain illnesses such as Alzheimer's disease and Parkinson's disease is not.

Hospitalization Requirement. Some policies will only cover nursing home costs, for example, if the individual was hospitalized first.

The Length of Coverage. How long is your parent covered under the policy? The average benefit is for a 3-year stay in a nursing home.

Inflation Protection. Under some policies, your benefits are adjusted for inflation (5% per year) but your premium remains the same. You might get a lower premium if you opt for no inflation protection, but this could result in a payment gap when the coverage is needed.

The Nonforfeiture Benefit. Some policies now offer some form of nonforfeiture benefit. Under certain conditions, there will be some residual benefit when the LTC policy lapses or you die. The nonforfeiture benefit can take at least two forms:

- The insurer will return a certain percentage of the premiums you have paid (minus any benefits you have received) when you either terminate the policy or die
- You may be entitled to a smaller benefit amount if the policy lapses after being in force for a minimum number of years

Your E&Y Planner Says:

It generally doesn't make sense to think about a long-term care policy until you are in your mid- to late 50s. The drawback to waiting until older age to buy a policy, however, is that your parents (or you, if the coverage is for you) may not be insurable at that time and/or the premiums may be very costly.

    You should calculate the cost of a policy over the period when you will be paying the premiums, and then calculate the potential cost of paying for a nursing home or other long-term care out of your or your parents' assets instead. Assess the probability and determine if you or your parents could afford simply to pay these costs if needed later. Then you can decide whether to purchase long-term care insurance or to self-insure for this cost by using your or your parents' assets. You could even earmark some savings now that would be used later if needed for this purpose.

Your Parents' Finances

Talking about the need for a will with your parents isn't easy. "Everything we have is yours," they may say. If only life—and financial planning—were so easy. Drawing up some basic financial plans with your parents while they're still active and in good health is essential, however, because it ensures that their wishes will be understood should they die or become incapacitated. A simple discussion now about their finances could alleviate much stress and confusion later on.

The Importance of a Will. Your parents have probably already had their wills drawn up and revised. If not, now's the time to do it. Depending upon the size of your estate and your parents' estate, you may want to coordinate your parents' will with your own. This may save you, your parents, and your children money in the long run.

Some grandparents, for instance, bequeath their estates directly to their grandchildren in the hopes of saving on estate taxes. Each person can leave up to $1 million in a generation-skipping trust for his or her grandchildren. Even though the parents (you) can use the trust assets if needed, those assets will not be taxed in the parents' estates. (See the case study "When Your Children Can't Leave Home" earlier in this chapter for a complete explanation.) If your parents have a sizable estate, it is clearly important for them to plan carefully and to coordinate their plans with your own situation and planning.

Providing Day-to-Day Support. If your parents need a little extra cash to cover their expenses, you should think about how best to provide that assistance. If you simply give them the cash as needed, your support is generally considered a gift. You don't have to report the amount on a gift tax return unless your gifts exceed $10,000 to each parent per year (or $20,000 combined). If you are married or have a life partner, you and your husband/partner can each give $10,000 to each of your parents without having to report any gifts. That means you could give as much as $40,000 in one year. If you are single and supporting only one parent, the amount you can gift tax free is limited to $10,000 per year. In addition, these tax-free gift amounts can pay for your parents' medical expenses and be subject to no gift tax (as long as you pay the expenses directly rather than reimbursing your parents for the costs they incur).

If you are providing more than 50% of your parents' support each year (and you meet other criteria), you can claim your parents as dependents on your tax return and can take a deduction for them (just as you would for a dependent child).

Another alternative is to give your parents a loan—with or without interest—that will be repaid at some specific time or event, such as when they sell their house. If the cumulative loans are more than $10,000, you generally must report interest payments as taxable income on your tax return—even if you don't charge interest. The IRS generally imputes interest on family loans at the prime rate.

Another technique to consider if your parents are reluctant to take money from you: a reverse mortgage. Under this arrangement, the bank pays your parents an annuity each month until they sell their home or die, at which time the bank would be repaid (with interest) out of the proceeds of the sale of the home. However, make sure you carefully evaluate all the fees and understand all of the details of the reverse mortgage before taking one out. To make this more palatable to your parents, you might set up your own reverse mortgage. You would pay them a monthly amount during their lifetimes, and you would get their home at their deaths.

Who Will Manage Your Parents' Affairs If They Can't? The day may come when your parents are no longer capable of managing their own affairs. That's why they should execute two other important documents: a durable power of attorney for all legal and financial matters and a health care power of attorney. These legal arrangements authorize a spouse, relative, close friend, or trusted advisor to make financial, legal, and health care decisions if the person granting the power is no longer able to do so. If your parents don't have such a document, and one of them becomes incapacitated, your family might have to go to court to secure the appointment of a guardian, or conservator, who will then manage the ailing parent's affairs. Most important, power of attorney documents let your mother and father decide in advance who will make decisions for them if they are unable to do so themselves.

Most states permit people to execute "springing" powers of attorney. These powers won't spring into action unless needed. The person given the power can only act after incapacity occurs. The advantage to this arrangement: Your parents (or you) do not have to worry about their children (whom they want to take care of their portfolio if they become incapacitated) messing around in their financial matters under ordinary circumstances. The disadvantage: The attorney-in-fact (you) must prove that your parents are incapacitated to be able to act on their behalf.

Typically, couples grant each other power of attorney; if both are deemed incapable of managing their affairs, a successor (generally you or one of your siblings) is named. Your parents do not have to name the same people on each document. Once these documents have been drawn up, make sure that you (or whoever is named on the document) and your parents' attorney each have copies of the document.

Your parents might also want to consider executing a living will. This document lets them specify their desires about being kept alive by artificial life support equipment and when to stop medical treatment during a terminal illness.

The Location of Important Documents. It's not uncommon for your parents to have savings accounts and other investments you don't know about. To simplify matters for the future, ask your parents to compile a complete list of their assets and liabilities, noting the location of the documents related to these items. (For instance, "my will is in a vault at ABC law firm; my stock certificates are held by the XYZ brokerage.") Be sure your parents include a copy of their will(s); all bank account and investment records; Social Security records, including their Social Security numbers; insurance policies; pension records; and mortgage papers as well as the telephone numbers of their attorneys, accountants, and financial advisors. Either you or a trusted legal advisor should keep a copy of this list. If your parents wish to maintain their privacy, they can send you one list in a "Do-Not-Open-Until" box or a similar secure place.

Preparing for the Inevitable. One last chore that you may need to assist your parents with is helping them select a burial site. Making these plans while they are still healthy will give them—and you—some peace of mind. It may also save on expenses at the time of your parents' deaths by avoiding pressured decisions that follow the death of a loved one. (See Chapter 7 for a discussion of funeral costs and decisions.)

As one client stated during our planning session for her elderly in-laws: "My husband just gets too angry with his parents, both of whom are in their 80s. He does not have patience for their temerity and the slow pace at which they make choices. It makes him feel awkward to talk about their medical costs and their financial situation. He's out of the picture now, and I'm working out their finances on my own."

LOOKING AHEAD:
What You Should Be Doing Right Now

1. When your children are young, decide if you will live on one income or two. Consider the effect of taxes on that second salary and the additional costs associated with working as well as the long-term effects of one spouse stepping out of the workforce.
2. As a parent, you need a will because it designates your child's guardian.
3. As the parent of dependent children, you must reevaluate your life, disability, and health insurance coverage.
4. Think about setting up a fund for your child's college education as soon as possible. The more years you have before he or she goes to college, the more time your investment will have to grow and the less money you may actually have to save as a result.
5. If you believe your aging parents will need long-term care in the future, you may want to consider buying a long-term care insurance policy.
6. Assist your parents now in preparing their wills, powers of attorney, health care proxies, and the like.
7. Help your parents with the difficult decisions regarding where they will be buried.

6

DEALING WITH DIVORCE

FACT — One-Quarter of All Divorced Women in America Live at or below the Poverty Level*

FACT — After a No-Fault Divorce, the Average Man's Standard of Living Goes Up 23% While the Average Woman's Standard of Living Goes Down 10%*

Divorce is always devastating. The process of untangling two lives is emotionally wrenching for spouses, children, family, and friends. But divorce is also traumatic from a financial perspective. You have legal fees. He has legal fees. And now you're no longer two living as cost-effectively as one. Instead, you have separate homes with separate utility, maintenance, and grocery bills.

No one gets married thinking they may eventually divorce, but the fact is that nearly half of all new marriages currently end in divorce.

Making Change by Neale S. Godfrey, Simon & Schuster, 1997.

And when couples split up, it's often the woman who loses out financially. Many women discover, for instance, that their standard of living declines after a divorce. For a woman who has never held a paying job, knowing that your support will end can be a frightening proposition. Also, for a woman who has been out of the job market for many years, getting back to full-time paid employment can be a daunting prospect.

The biggest obstacle in a divorce proceeding, though, may be your own mind-set. You may convince yourself that this is just a temporary situation, that your differences can be reconciled.

If ever there were a perfect time for financial planning, it's now. You must force yourself to face the situation and get your finances in order. With enough money in hand, you can hopefully pick up the pieces and start over again.

If Divorce Is a Possibility

Your marriage may truly be on the verge of collapsing—or you may have simply hit a rough spot in your life together. Whatever your situation, you might think it best to sit and wait for further developments. But that strategy could leave you vulnerable. While you're waiting and deciding, your husband may be taking steps to secure his own financial situation. Perhaps you and your husband will ultimately work things out; perhaps you won't. Unfortunately, you can't predict what will happen, so what you need to do now is get organized. Taking this first step doesn't mean you've set the divorce proceedings in motion and there's no turning back. Nor does it rule out a change of heart on your part or a reconciliation. It simply means that no matter what happens, you'll be ready. Ironically, sometimes looking at the financial aspects of divorce encourages reconciliation.

Consult with an Attorney

You need some advice from an objective third party. Consulting with an attorney doesn't necessarily mean you and your husband will divorce. A matrimonial lawyer will simply tell you what to expect—and advise you about alimony, custody, and property settlement issues. Not only men pay alimony: Some wives pay alimony and child support to their husbands. An attorney may also suggest some strategies to protect your assets.

If you don't have an attorney, ask friends, relatives, and colleagues for a recommendation, especially if those people have gone through a divorce themselves. (See Chapter 11 for more information about selecting an attorney.) You want an attorney who specializes in matrimonial law. Some people are ultimately able to forgo attorney fees and represent themselves, or they use a mediator. If mediation or self-representation doesn't work, however, it's always advisable to consult an attorney to determine your rights and understand your options.

A do-it-yourself divorce generally involves filing the necessary documents at the clerk's office at the courthouse and appearing before the judge at a hearing to explain why you want a divorce. This procedure works best if you and your husband are not contesting the division of marital property, if you don't have any children, and if you haven't been married more than a couple of years.

Generally, it's wise to seek legal counsel at least for a consultation before you start the divorce proceeding. This is an emotionally charged time in your life, and it is only natural not to be able to focus on the details and the fine points.

Find Out What You're Worth

You must put a dollar figure on your joint assets and liabilities. You may think this is obvious—that you know what you own and what you owe—but one spouse may have investments or bank accounts of which the other spouse is unaware, and often one spouse handles all the financial details of the marriage. You may know, for instance, that your husband has a pension plan at work, but you may not know its value. You should. You may be eligible for part of that pension at some future date if it's built into your divorce agreement. Understanding your husband's pension plan also gives you an idea of what he can expect his income to be during retirement.

List all of your husband's bank accounts and your bank accounts as well as your other financial interests, such as an IRA, 401(k), profit sharing plan, pension plan, stocks, bonds, and real estate holdings. Name them and give their current value. Take inventory of your possessions. Include your home, cars, electronic equipment, and furniture. You may need a professional appraisal for antiques and jewelry. Don't forget to include the contents of your safe deposit box.

Once you have determined your assets, list them in three separate categories: joint or community property assets, your assets, and his assets. Think about which items you brought into the marriage and which items you purchased jointly. If your husband handled the family finances in your marriage, ask to review his files and papers for check stubs, receipts, bank statements, and tax returns. You will need as much documentation as possible to support your claims as to what assets exist, the valuation of those assets, and the source of funds used to acquire those assets.

> ### Your E&Y Planner Says:
>
> If your marriage is on the rocks, acquire all new assets in your own name if possible. In most cases, it's best to postpone such purchases (if possible) and keep your available cash in a separate account.

Make a list of your liabilities as well. What are your debts? Your husband's? Your joint debts? In general, it's easier to assess your liabilities than your assets because you get monthly statements to show the amount of debt. But if you are having trouble figuring out your liabilities, call the creditors directly to find out the amount owed. For a list of your creditors, contact one of the three national credit rating companies: Equifax, Experian, and Trans Union Corp. (See "Your Credit Report" in Chapter 1 for more information.) They'll send you a credit report that will list all of your current creditors.

FACT

You May Be Entitled to Social Security Benefits Based on Your Husband's Account—even if You're Divorced

If you and your ex-husband were married for at least 10 years—and if you are at least 62 years of age and currently unmarried—you're eligible to receive benefits on your ex-husband's Social Security record if he is receiving Social Security benefits (or is deceased). If your ex-husband has not applied for benefits, but can qualify for them and is age 62 or older, you can receive benefits on his record if you have been divorced from him for at least 2 years. Any benefits payable to you do not affect those payable to your ex-husband's current wife or minor children. Many women get a higher benefit based on their ex-husband's work record than they get on their own record, especially if he is deceased, but it depends on how much he has earned and contributed versus your own earnings and contributions. For your particular situation, you need to check with the Social Security Administration.

Open Your Own Checking Account

While it's always recommended that a woman maintain a separate bank account and at least one credit card for her own personal financial well-being, that advice is especially critical if divorce is likely. You need your own credit history so that if you are living on your own in the future, you will be able to get a new credit card or apply for a mortgage. (See Chapter 1 for more details on the importance of your own credit history.)

If you are separated from your husband but not yet divorced, it's generally advised that you change the signature authority on any joint accounts so that both of you must sign in order for any transaction to occur. (If your husband doesn't know you're intending to initiate a divorce, this is a clear indication of your intentions to take some sort of action.) With joint brokerage accounts, tell your broker in writing that no withdrawals are permitted without sign-off by both parties.

Your Current Living Expenses

As a single woman, and possibly a single mother, your daily financial picture will change dramatically. What are your current living expenses? How much do you spend on your children? How much do you anticipate spending on them in the future? Can you afford to maintain this lifestyle? Will you need to go back to work or find a better-paying job? Can you cut back on some expenses? Not only will keeping track of your income and expenses help you devise a postdivorce budget, it's also necessary in determining child custody and alimony payments. (See Chapter 1 for a budget worksheet.)

If you aren't working now, consider your options. Do you need to go back to school or get some retraining? Although you may have had a great job 10 years ago, it's unlikely that you'll just fall into a similar position today. You may have to pitch your resume in a new light. If you've been active in the school PTA or some other volunteer work, for instance, include those responsibilities—even though you didn't get paid for that job. And by all means, talk up your need for a job with everyone you know. Use the Internet (if you have access), scan the help wanted ads, or find a headhunter. Many people now find jobs, or at least leads for promising jobs, this way.

You may also want to seek professional help by going to a job counselor. She or he can help you position yourself for the current employment market. A job counselor can also help you determine what your interests and skills are so that you won't simply accept the first job that's offered to you. Rather, you'll look for a position that offers career advancement and financial remuneration. If you've been a homemaker, you can ask your attorney to include your training and counseling costs as part of your settlement.

Your E&Y Planner Says:

If you haven't been working, should you get a job before the divorce is final? This question always comes up. Often, women worry that if they get a job now and are earning a salary, they'll be awarded less in alimony and child support. That's generally true. But by getting a job, I believe you'll be coming out ahead. You will gain a greater sense of independence and self-worth, and you will get out in the world and meet new people. In addition, it's very likely that you will wind up with more money in hand. Your salary plus the amount that you receive in alimony and/or child support will, in most cases, be more than the amount of alimony and/or child support you would have received if you were not employed.

Of course, money isn't the only issue to consider. How will your children be affected by your return to paid employment? Unless you have very young babies at home, I've always found that women who are going through the emotional throes of divorce need to get out of the house. If a full-time job seems like too much too soon, look for part-time employment as a start. Or, take a course or go for training that will better prepare you for the job market when you are ready—or need—to go back to work.

Sizing Up a Business

If you and/or your husband own a family business, that's just as much a marital asset as your home or your bank accounts. In fact, a business is often the most valuable asset that a couple owns. If you are heading for a divorce, it's essential that you get an accurate valuation of the business before you start negotiating so that you can seek an equitable buyout. To determine the value of the company, you need to know how much the company is worth today, what the expectations for future growth are, and for which liabilities or debts you are responsible. You will probably need to hire a professional appraiser to do this. (Ask your attorney or accountant for a recommendation. Or contact the American Society of Appraisers at 800-272-8258, www.appraisers.org. They'll give you a list of accredited appraisers in your area.) You may find your appraiser determines a different value from your husband's appraiser.

How the business will be divided depends on who owns it, as well as the state in which you live. As with other assets, you can sell the business (and divide the proceeds), or one of you will keep the business and the other will get another asset, such as the house, the boat, or the IRAs. Or, one of you may want to buy the other out.

Your E&Y Planner Says:

If you filed joint tax returns with your ex-husband prior to this year, you would have been liable for any tax misrepresentation. However, as of July 22, 1998, a law became effective that makes it easier for divorced women to prove they were innocent of any tax misrepresentation of which they were unaware.

> According to the law, if you can prove that you didn't know the taxes were unpaid, if you are divorced, legally separated, or have lived apart for 12 months, you can elect to compute your own tax liability from the years in question based on your own income. You have 2 years after the IRS tries to collect from you to make this election. To better understand how this new law works, you may want to contact the IRS or a tax specialist.

Review Your Insurance

You are probably covered under either your husband's employee benefits plan or yours. Make sure you understand what type of health, disability, and life insurance coverage you have. You should carry more life and disability insurance on yourself since you can no longer rely on your husband's income. (See Chapter 5 for more details on assessing your life insurance needs.) Typical divorce settlements specify that the children are beneficiaries of your ex-husband's life insurance. Often the spouse who receives alimony is named the beneficiary of a life insurance policy as well until the alimony payments stop.

If you are covered by your husband's company health plan, you should be able to continue the same health coverage for at least 18 months under the Consolidated Omnibus Reconciliation Act (COBRA). You must pay the premiums, which may be costly. (Health coverage is sometimes negotiable with alimony or as part of the child support settlement.) After that, you are responsible for securing your own health insurance. If you're employed but don't currently use your company-sponsored plan, think about signing up. Group rates are usually far cheaper than an individual policy purchased on your own. Although employers don't generally let you sign up for insurance midyear, they will if the change is due to a "life event," such as death, divorce, marriage, or the birth of a child. Continuation of health coverage for the children, and you, is often one of the many points that are negotiated during a divorce proceeding.

Now is the time to change the beneficiaries on your life insurance policies, and retirement plan accounts, too. If something should happen to you during this holding period, and you don't want your estranged husband to get your assets, take his name off as beneficiary on any accounts on which he's listed. You will most probably want your children to be beneficiaries of your life insurance policy. If you have an IRA, change the beneficiary. If you have a tax-deferred savings or retirement plan through your employer, you may not be able to change the beneficiary designation. For a 401(k) plan, you need spousal consent to change the beneficiary, as your spouse is the automatic beneficiary. If your husband has power of attorney over any separate savings or checking accounts that are in your name only, change those too. It's easy to overlook these important financial planning details when there's so much to think about. But think of the possible consequences if you don't: Should you die suddenly, your ex-husband would inherit the full amount in your 401(k) plan or other tax-deferred savings plan.

MEETING WITH YOUR ATTORNEY

Good legal advice is generally expensive. Attorneys bill you for every letter written, every phone call made, every minute spent filing papers in court. So do the things you can by yourself. In a divorce case, you need to gather an incredible amount of financial data. A quick glance through your checkbook and brokerage accounts, for instance, will give you a substantial amount of information. Some documents you should gather yourself include:

1. *Your income tax returns.* A trail to most of your assets flows through your tax return. You need copies of your income tax returns for at least 3 years (or longer, if there's been a substantial change in your tax situation), preferably with the supporting documents used to prepare those tax returns such as W-2 and 1099 forms, bank and brokerage statements, and copies of checks for real estate taxes.
2. *One of your husband's paycheck stubs.* This will show his current income and withholding to use for the settlement proceedings.
3. *Copies of your husband's employee benefits statements.* (You will need yours too, but those are easy to get. Just contact the human resources department where you work.) These statements will show how much your soon-to-be ex-husband is contributing to his pension and other

employer-sponsored plans as well as outline the health, disability, and life insurance benefits that his employer provides. Review prior statements to make sure that any disbursements from these accounts are above board—and not money your husband is squirreling away in a separate bank account. Keep in mind that any distributions from plans not made to joint beneficiaries should have been signed off by you. You need to follow up if you see any large disbursements paid to institutions with which you are unfamiliar.

4. *Your wish list.* Make a list of the assets that you want to keep—no matter what.

5. *A record of the children's activities.* Keep track of how much time you spend with the children and what types of activities you do. This will help if you are fighting over custody. Tracking expenses will help you determine how much alimony and income you will need.

FACT | **You Are Generally Entitled to a Portion of Your Ex-husband's Retirement Benefits If They Were Earned by Your Ex during Your Marriage**

To get your share of your ex-husband's retirement nest egg, your lawyer must petition a state court for a qualified domestic relations order (QDRO). This court order will tell the pension plan administrator how to divide the benefits between you and your ex-husband. You can generally receive your share of the money as monthly payments at retirement or as a lump-sum payment you can roll over into your own IRA. The money you receive from the splitting of the account is not taxable if rolled into another qualified retirement plan. When you withdraw the funds, it will be taxable.

A CASE STUDY: THE STORY OF LAURA WILLIAMS

People frequently consult with an attorney when they are contemplating divorce. But you can also speak with one of your financial advisers for some general guidance. Over the years, I've counseled a number of cases such as the following:

Before Laura even sat down in my office, she asked if she could pay me in cash—and pulled out a stack of bills. I assured her that one form of money was as good as another. (Secretly I wondered how I'd explain this to accounts payable!)

"It's just that I don't want my husband to know I'm talking to you," Laura said breathlessly. I told her that I thought it would be unlikely he'd find out. (Although conversations about tax matters with CPAs have some protection now under new law, financial planning discussions are generally not protected the way that conversations with attorneys and physicians are.)

She glanced over her shoulder, and began her story.

Laura's marriage was shaky. Her career had taken off, while her husband, Alan, was basically treading water. After the birth of their twins 3 years earlier, Alan had decided to quit his job and stay at home full time to raise their daughters. Laura was free to work longer hours and travel more.

As unconventional as this arrangement may seem to some people, I've seen it work perfectly well for a number of couples. Unfortunately, it was not working well for Laura and Alan. Alan was tired of his stay-at-home role, so the previous month he had asked Laura to leave her job and assume his job at home. Laura didn't want to. And Alan refused to leave the girls with a nanny, citing the horror stories in the press. Both Laura and Alan felt the marriage was in jeopardy.

Laura was especially frightened by Alan's threat to leave her, take the girls, and sue for primary custody, alimony, and child support. Could he legally do this? she asked. I suggested that Laura discuss the matter thoroughly with a divorce attorney. But the short answer was that a nonworking spouse who had assumed primary care of the children generally had rights to both alimony and child support. It didn't matter if that spouse was male or female. And, although mothers generally are awarded primary custody more frequently than fathers, more and more fathers are winning custody.

Laura was also concerned about the ownership of a valuable art collection she had inherited from her grandmother. Alan had also threatened to ask for half of it in any divorce settlement. In general, inherited property, when it is kept separate (as it had been, in this case) is not regarded as marital property.

Most of Laura's other assets were held jointly with Alan. The only exception: her retirement accounts and company stock options. Would these be divided too? she asked. Probably, but it depends on state law. In community property states like Texas, where Laura and Alan lived, each spouse would most likely get half.

Laura didn't know what to do. I suggested that she build separate accounts for herself over the next few months so that if she and her husband split up, the process would be less difficult for her.

That's one of the ironic things about planning for divorce. Marriage is built on trust, but divorce needs caution. What you do to improve your chances for a quick and easy divorce may damage your chances for a reconciliation.

Fortunately, that wasn't the case for Laura and Alan. Reviewing their current situation worked wonders. Soon thereafter, the girls started nursery school. Alan finally had some time to launch his own business from home, and Laura continued to climb the corporate ladder.

THE BASIC ELEMENTS OF A DIVORCE

The actual divorce proceeding is all about claiming what's yours, whether it's the house and the boat, full custody of the children or pets, or a share of a sizable pension fund or retirement savings. The combination of these elements—a property settlement, child support, and alimony—is very intertwined. It's like a jigsaw puzzle. One piece is the division of assets; another piece is the alimony payment that provides for both spouse and the kids; and the final piece is child support, which is for the children's welfare alone.

THE PROPERTY SETTLEMENT

Marriage is a partnership. Any property acquired during the marriage, by either spouse, is *marital* property (according to most state laws). *Separate* property, on the other hand, is property that each spouse acquired before the marriage, after separation, or through an inheritance or gift during the marriage (as long as it has not been commingled with marital property). In the event of a divorce, marital property must be divided. Generally, this is done according to the laws of the state in which you are living at the time of the divorce so, while reading the information in this chapter, keep in mind that you must consult an attorney.

There are two basic ways to divide marital property: *community property* settlement and *equitable distribution of property* settlement. A third, called *common-law* settlement, is applicable only in Mississippi. Under common law, property goes to the person whose name is on it. If the deed to the house is in your husband's name, he gets it.

Nine states use the concept of community property to divide marital assets. Under these rules, all the property and assets acquired during the marriage are split 50-50 between you and your husband. The community property states are Arizona, California, Idaho, Louisiana, Nevada, New Mexico, Texas, Washington, and Wisconsin.

Equitable distribution applies in the remaining states (except Mississippi) and the District of Columbia. Under these rules, the court decides on an "equitable" distribution of your assets. This is not necessarily a 50-50 split. Nor does *equitable* always mean *fair*. The court will consider various factors, such as how long you were married, your earning potential, your age and health, who has custody of the children, and your financial need, in determining who gets the house, the car, and so forth.

But it is very difficult, even for the best of judges, to decide how much you and your husband each deserve to take away from the marriage. For instance, what if you stayed at home for the past 10 years to take care of the kids while your husband continued to work for a living? Let's imagine further that your husband has been rather successful in his career: a few choice promotions, a comfortable six-figure salary, and a sizable pension plan. How much do you think he will easily give up? How much do you feel is your rightful share? It can be equally difficult to get a piece of a smaller amount of assets. Even if you and your spouse have moderate assets, your husband will understandably want to keep as much as he can.

Until recently, most women who found themselves in similar circumstances were advised to determine how much they needed to live comfortably and to ask for that amount rather than to hold out for what they believed was their due. But that strategy isn't adopted across the board anymore. Some spouses are seeking a share of their mate's employee benefits, such as stock options, which previously were not considered marital property.

None of this matters, of course, if you signed a prenuptial agreement that is binding and legal. (For more details on prenuptial agreements, see

Chapter 2.) You can always contest the validity of a prenup, but it would be advisable to seek a divorce attorney's counsel before doing so.

> ### Your E&Y Planner Says:
>
> In many divorce proceedings, the wife may ask for the family home as part of her settlement so that she can maintain a sense of continuity and stability for herself and her children. That plan works fine—if you can afford it on your new postdivorce budget. But many new divorcées cannot. One idea is to get your husband to agree to pay the mortgage and real estate taxes for at least some period of time. This could be included in the divorce agreement. Otherwise, in order to keep the house, you may have to really struggle to make ends meet. You will now be paying the mortgage, taxes, insurance, and upkeep from a combination of your own salary, alimony, and child support payments. You may find yourself using your credit cards more often, paying just the minimum balance when the bill comes due. You may even cut back on your 401(k) contribution so that your paycheck is slightly higher. In the end, you may wind up with less savings and more debt—and you may be forced to sell the house anyway. If keeping the family home is going to set you back financially, move to a smaller house or an apartment after the divorce. The kids will adjust. You and your children may even find (as many do when they sell the house a few years later) that you really benefit from a change of location and a fresh start.

ALIMONY

Alimony is the amount of money your ex-husband is required to pay you—or you are required to pay him—under a divorce or separation agreement. It is taxable income for the person receiving it. The person paying alimony, however, can take a tax deduction for any payments.

If you will be receiving alimony, how much you will get depends upon the rules of the state in which you live. All states consider both need and earning power when determining an amount. But some states also take into account the length of the marriage.

Alimony can continue for any term of years. A spouse may receive alimony for just the first few years following a divorce. Or, no alimony may be awarded. Typically, there won't be much or any alimony if there is a substantial property settlement or if you and your spouse have comparable incomes. In some cases, of course, a spouse could be awarded alimony for life.

If you've never worked outside the home or if your income has been smaller than your husband's—and if you have been married for a long time—you will most likely be entitled to alimony. It may be rehabilitative (that is, for a limited period of time) or permanent. The pendulum has swung back and forth on the issue of permanent alimony. To find out what your chances of receiving it (or paying it) are, talk with your attorney about recent state precedent.

In almost every case, alimony stops if one spouse dies, or if the alimony recipient remarries or starts cohabiting with someone. These cohabitation clauses have become fairly prevalent in the past few years. Basically, they prevent a spouse from continuing to collect support if he or she is essentially living as husband or wife with another person. In many cases, if you or your ex-husband has been living with a new partner for 30 consecutive days over a 12-month period, that qualifies as co-habitating.

Your E&Y Planner Says:

You can get a lump-sum settlement instead of monthly alimony payments. For some spouses, that's a good idea, because you don't have to worry about your ex-husband sending you your payment each month. And, if you decide to move in with someone else, your payments can't be cut off because of a cohabitation clause—you already have the money in hand. But many women like the idea of getting a steady income each month. It's forced budgeting and gives a sense of security. Of course, this ignores the fact that many ex-spouses don't pay the alimony and/or child support to which they have committed. Your former spouse may resist this arrangement because he cannot take a tax deduction with a lump-sum settlement.

The Spouse Who Pays Alimony Cannot Forgo Child Support in Lieu of More Alimony

But he or she can pay substantially more in alimony than in child support—if he or she requests it. Many spouses who pay alimony prefer this payment structure because alimony payments are tax deductible and child support payments are not.

You or Your Spouse Can Get Temporary Alimony

If you and your husband are legally separated, you or he can usually get the court to require *pendente lite,* or temporary, support. This may be used as a precedent for settling alimony and child support payments.

➤ *Your E&Y Planner Says:*

If you are entitled to alimony and/or child support, make sure your spouse carries a sufficient amount of disability and life insurance coverage that names you or your children as the beneficiary. That way you have some protection in case your husband can no longer earn a salary and thus can't make support payments to you for an extended period of time (or, in the case of his death when payments will stop).

CHILD SUPPORT

Every state has its own guidelines for determining the appropriate amount of child support for divorcing parents. Some states, for instance, calculate support payments by estimating your child's standard of living and dividing that figure by your total family income. In this situation, either you or your ex-husband could be asked to pay 100% of your child's support if one of you is a stay-at-home parent. Other states may require that a certain percentage of your or your ex-husband's income go toward child support, even if you both are working.

Support payments generally last until your child reaches the age of majority. (That's age 18 to 21, depending on the state in which you live.) To get your former spouse to pay child support, you may have to take him to court. One woman followed her ex-husband, who owed her a substantial amount in unpaid child support, from New York to Vermont. He had used several different aliases. Eventually, the state arrested him and forced him to pay the support. Today, the courts are growing increasingly sympathetic to women's complaints about deadbeat dads. Most states now have a wage garnishment program, which will take unpaid child support payments directly from an ex-spouse's paycheck.

Both alimony and child support may be reduced, however, if the spouse who is paying the alimony loses his or her job or suffers a severe financial setback. In some situations, a spouse can collect back alimony payments and/or claim increased alimony or child support payments. If you or your former husband gets a new job that pays considerably more than you or he earned previously, it is unlikely that alimony payments will be boosted, though. By definition, that additional salary is either yours or your husband's alone because it was earned after the marriage ended.

Unlike alimony, child support payments are not tax deductible for your spouse. Nor are they considered taxable income for you. If you're applying for credit, however, the alimony and child support payments you receive are considered cash flow and will be added as income when calculating how much debt you can handle. Alimony and child support will also be considered cash flow by colleges reviewing your child's application for financial aid.

LOOKING AHEAD:
What You Should Be Doing Right Now

Whether you're contemplating divorce or in the midst of a divorce proceeding, you should:

1. *Consult with an attorney.* Pick a professional who specializes in matrimonial law.

2. *Calculate your net worth.* Which assets qualify as marital assets? Which as nonmarital? How much debt do you owe?

3. *Open your own checking account.* It's a good idea for every woman to have her own account even in the best situations.

4. *Calculate your current living expenses.* Once you see the bottom line, you may have to cut your expenses or get some additional training to qualify for a higher-paying job.

5. *Review your insurance.* Will you and the kids still be covered by your former spouse's health insurance plan? Reconsider your life and disability insurance needs and beneficiary designations.

6. *Find out what the property distribution laws are in your state.* Property is divided differently in equitable distribution states compared to community property states. (If you live in Mississippi, make sure assets are not solely in your spouse's name.)

7

WIDOWHOOD: THE BASICS

Losing your spouse after a lifetime together—or even after a short time—is emotionally devastating. Unfortunately, at a time when you need solitude to grieve and find peace of mind, the real world intrudes. How you handle your financial situation is crucial to your well-being for years to come.

Six months after he retired, my father died suddenly of a heart attack. My mother, who had always expected my father to outlive her, was shocked—and completely unprepared.

After the funeral, we spent several days sifting through an enormous pile of paperwork. Condolence letters and gifts needed to be acknowledged. Funeral bills needed to be paid. Attorney's forms needed to be filled out. Bank accounts needed to be changed. Finally, my mother looked up from a note she was writing and said, "I'm so busy taking care of this stuff that I don't have time to sit and think about your father. And I really need to do that."

My mother was right.

The death of your husband or life partner is one of the most traumatic experiences you'll ever face. It's a tremendous personal and emotional loss that can leave you feeling confused, exhausted, and alone. The last thing that you'll want to worry about is sorting through your husband's estate and filing the necessary paperwork.

But when your husband dies (either unexpectedly, like my father, or after a long illness) a woman generally can't just sit and grieve. Like so many other critical points in your life, the death of a loved one raises financial concerns that must be addressed—if not immediately, then over the next several days, weeks, and/or months.

Should I use my husband's life insurance settlement to pay off my mortgage? Am I eligible for any benefits? Can I afford to retire? Those are the kinds of questions you'll need to answer. As a widow, you must now make financial decisions on your own about everything from repairing a leaky roof (or replacing it) to selling the house and buying your car when the lease is up.

The situation can prove troublesome if your husband handled the financial matters in your marriage and you now have to wrestle with the weekly household budget, save for the children's college education, and plan your own retirement. If you've been a stay-at-home mother, you may now have to think about returning to paid employment. Will you need to update your skills? Who will care for the children when you're not at home? If your husband left a large estate, you may have to decide how best to invest the proceeds as well as how to bequeath the remainder to your heirs. Should you set up a living trust, for instance, or a testamentary trust? In some cases, you may simply have to pay the bills and balance a checkbook for the first time in your life.

Like many wives, you may not be prepared to deal with any of these matters, especially in the early days following your husband's death. You will probably have trouble making up your mind (even if you're normally a quick decision-maker). People will say things to you three or four times before you hear them. And you won't have your usual amount of energy or ambition. If possible, you might want to seek some emotional support from a grief counselor, therapist, or support group. (Your church or temple should be able to make some recommendations for you. If not, ask friends or relatives. Or call the employee assistance program at your office, if such a program is available. Grief is one of the many problems they're trained to help you deal with.) Once you have a support system in place, you will be able to tackle the tasks at hand. Over time, you *will* begin to pick up the pieces and to slowly get on with your life. You'll remember it's what your husband would want for you.

Friends, family members, even co-workers will offer assistance and guidance during this time. Accept what help you can. But bear in mind that even those people with the best of intentions may not be as knowledgeable as they appear. Any poorly informed advice could lead you to make a hasty or bad decision. As a rule of thumb, don't make any major decisions about your house, your car, your insurance, your investments, or your family without thinking things over for at least a few days. Talk it over with someone you trust, and think seriously about consulting an attorney or a financial planner. If a decision can wait until next month or next year, then by all means wait.

In the meantime, put all of your husband's mail (there'll be plenty of it) into a large box you can sort through later on and concentrate on accomplishing the following tasks:

YOUR TO DO LIST: RIGHT AWAY

1. Notify family and friends.
2. Read your husband's letter of instruction (if there is one). Besides telling you where you'll find his will and the key to his safe deposit box, it may also outline his wishes regarding a funeral service.
3. Make funeral arrangements. (See the boxed section later in this chapter.)
4. Find the will (if there is one). If your husband has died without a will (it's called dying intestate), an administrator will be appointed by the court. (See the section entitled "Understanding Probate" later in this chapter.)
5. Call your attorney. If you don't have one, ask friends for references. Obviously you can handle much of this work yourself, but at the very least you need an attorney to call for occasional advice or should problems arise. In this case, you don't necessarily want the lawyer who handled your cousin's divorce. You need an attorney who specializes in trusts and estates.
6. If you are going to use an attorney to do part or all of the administration for the estate, ask him or her to quote you a fixed fee. Hourly fees can really dig a hole in your funds.
7. Make sure you have enough cash on hand. Your bank account may be temporarily frozen until probate gets under way. If you need

cash, you may have to make an emergency application to the estate for funds.

8. Upgrade the locks on the doors to your house or apartment or consider installing an alarm system. Why? Death notices published in the local newspaper can be seen as an open invitation by burglars.

9. Find out who the executor of your husband's estate is. Often, the widow is named as executor of her spouse's estate. In other cases, one or more of your grown children, your spouse's brother or sister, or a trusted friend will be named as executor.

10. Chances are, you're the executor. Therefore, you're responsible for settling the estate, which means beginning probate, listing the assets of the estate, paying the bills, settling the debts, filing the estate tax return, and—finally—distributing the assets of your husband's estate.

YOUR TO DO LIST: WITHIN THE MONTH

1. *Get a copy of your husband's death certificate.* You'll need several copies, in fact. (Your funeral director can get them for you.) Government agencies, insurance companies, and credit card issuers require proof that your husband died.

2. *Notify the bank or financial institution and credit card companies that your joint accounts need to be changed to your name only.*

3. *Contact your husband's creditors.* Ask that bills be sent to you or to the executor of the estate.

4. *Contact the Social Security Administration.* You can file a benefits claim by phone (800-772-1213), by computer (www.ssa.gov), or in person at a local office. In 1998, you were entitled to a $255 death benefit if you were married for at least 9 months prior to your husband's death. You can receive widows' benefits if you are age 60 or older. If you are a widow with children, you may be eligible for a widow's benefit at any age when you are caring for a child who is under age 16 or disabled and entitled to benefits. Unmarried children may receive survivors' benefits on your husband's record until they are age 18 (or age 19 if they are attending school full time).

5. *If your husband was working at the time of his death, notify his employer.* You may be due some money if your husband's employer offered life insurance. You'll want to find out about his pension. And ask about

medical insurance, too. The Consolidated Omnibus Budget Reconciliation Act (COBRA) gives you the right to keep your medical benefits under your husband's plan at work for up to 36 months. You'll have to pay the premiums, though, which may be expensive. The human resources department should be able to help you. (See the section entitled "Notify Your Husband's Employer" later in this chapter.)

6. *Contact the issuer(s) of your husband's life insurance policy(s).* You will probably need a copy of his death certificate, the policy number, the face value of the policy (the amount for which he was insured), and a copy of his birth certificate. Usually, you can elect to receive the proceeds of his insurance policy as a lump-sum payment or in installments over a certain period. Keep in mind that life insurance benefits are income tax free.

7. *Call or visit your local office of the Department of Veterans Affairs if your husband served in the military.* You may be eligible for a pension, and, in some cases, the government will pay some funeral and burial costs. You'll probably need a record of his military discharge papers.

8. *Change your insurance policies if your husband was the beneficiary.* (Change the beneficiary designation on your retirement accounts as well.) Reevaluate your own coverage. Do you need additional coverage? Do you need less coverage? This will vary according to whether or not you still have dependents.

9. *Revise and update your own will.* If you have minor children, make sure you name a guardian for them.

Notify Your Husband's Employer

As soon as possible, contact your husband's employer to report his death. If you notify his employer by phone, be sure to follow up with a letter. Ask about the following:

- Accrued but unpaid bonuses.
- Accrued but unpaid vacation time.
- Vested but unexercised stock options, including exercise procedures and time limits.

- Continuing benefits available to survivors, such as medical and dental coverage, life insurance, and so on.
- Rules and elections available for distributions from 401(k) and pension plans.
- Life insurance coverages and procedures for filing a claim.
- Your husband's last paystub. You need it for year-end tax planning.
- Family assistance programs available to surviving family members and ongoing employee discount programs available to survivors.
- An employee benefits booklet. It is useful to have a record you can refer to: In case the human resources representative forgets to tell you about a pertinent benefit, you can read about it yourself.

Making Final Arrangements

Many people don't make funeral arrangements in advance. Instead, they wait until the need arises—until a spouse or other loved one dies—before they make any final plans. That could lead you to overspend. At a time like this, you're thinking with your heart rather than your head.

Mortuaries operate like any other business. Most providers are reputable, but some will try to take advantage of this emotionally charged situation by shaming you into buying the "very best" for your loved one. Don't spend more than you had planned, though. Despite what the funeral director says, the amount you spend on a funeral and burial does not reflect how you felt about the deceased.

Although many people pick a funeral home based on its location, reputation, or the consumer's personal experience, it's not in bad taste to shop around for the best price. Call or visit at least two funeral homes and cemeteries to compare prices. On average, a traditional funeral costs $4,782, according to the National Funeral Directors Association, with an additional $2,400 for an in-ground burial. (By contrast, the average cost of a cremation is $1,300 nationwide.) By law (called the Funeral Rule), mortuaries must give prices to consumers by telephone or provide price lists at their facilities. (Cemeteries are not bound by the federal ruling, however.)

When comparing prices, make sure you're comparing costs for the entire package, not just a single item. Most funeral homes list prices for caskets, outer burial containers, and general funeral services separately. But you need to tally all three costs to reach your total. One firm may charge more for a casket, for example, but less for the funeral director's fee.

Caskets come in all styles and prices. Generally, they're made from metal, wood, fiberglass, or plastic and are the most expensive item in a traditional funeral. (A casket will run you about one-third of the total funeral bill.) An outer burial container, which surrounds the casket in the grave, is required by most cemeteries. The general funeral services tab includes the funeral director's fee, transportation of the body to the cemetery, and use of the facilities for a wake or visitation. Items that might cost extra include flowers, obituary notices, and music.

MYTH

Don't Worry about Paying Your Bills during Bereavement

The concerns of everyday life just seem to stop during periods of mourning. Telephone calls aren't returned. Letters aren't answered. And bills aren't paid. While it is tempting to waive aside such concerns until you've dealt with the funeral and your husband's estate has been settled, creditors aren't generally that understanding. There is no such thing as a bereavement grace period. Failure to pay your monthly credit card, telephone, and mortgage bills can result in substantial interest charges, late fees, and a damaged credit record. If you feel overwhelmed, it's best to get a family member or close friend to help make sure you pay your bills on time.

➤ *Your E&Y Planner Says:*

Burglars aren't the only ones reading the obituaries. In the weeks following your husband's death, you'll be plagued by one cold call after another from insurance agents, real estate brokers, and a host of salespeople who want to "help" you.

I spent the first month after my father died living with my mother. In those 30 days, she got more than 50 calls from salespeople. One insurance agent insisted she needed a new hospitalization policy, which we discovered after reading the fine print duplicated coverage that she already had. Realtors called with promises of instant buyers. Appraisers promised to correctly value the contents of her house. Brokers called to "help" her invest and manage her assets. Landscapers offered to mow her tiny lawn.

None of those 50 callers was peddling a single service that my mother needed. But they all had convincing stories. Fortunately, my mother and I soon sized up the situation—and were able to tell them to go away. If you can't say no to these unsolicited callers, however, ask them to send you some information. When it arrives, throw it in that catch-all box we suggested earlier. You can then peruse this material at your leisure. Or screen your phone calls if you have an answering machine until these solicitations start to drop off.

DEATH—AND TAXES

You will have to file a final federal and state income tax return for your husband for any income he earned up to the date of his death. It is not due until the traditional filing date of April 15, regardless of what time during the year your husband died. In addition, you may have to file an estate income tax return for income earned by his estate after the date of his death. The due date of this return will depend upon decisions made regarding the year-end of the estate.

If you have always filed a joint tax return, you can do that now as well—as long as you don't remarry before the end of the tax year. These returns can be tricky, so it's probably a good idea to seek professional advice from an accountant. Some things to be on the lookout for:

- *Medical costs.* These costs incurred by your husband the year of his death can be filed either on Schedule A of the 1040 or on the estate tax return, but not on both.
- *Estate expenses.* Funeral and probate costs belong on the estate tax return (Form 706), or estate income tax return (Form 1041), not on your husband's final income tax return (Form 1040).
- *Signatures.* On your income tax return, the executor or your attorney signs for your deceased husband. You sign for yourself.
- *Qualifying widow.* In the second year after your husband's death, you can file as a qualifying widow on your tax return. Thereafter, if you have dependents living at home, you can file as a head of household. In both cases, you will be taxed at lower married rather than higher single rates.

The federal government collects estate tax on estates worth more than $650,000 (in 1999). But your husband (assuming he is a U.S. citizen) can leave any amount of money to you, his wife, without incurring that federal estate tax. This is known as the unlimited marital deduction. When you die, however, you can't similarly pass that money tax-free to your children or another nonspouse beneficiary. The tax-free transfer is from spouse to spouse only.

To other family members and friends, your husband can leave up to $650,000 (in 1999) before a federal estate tax is levied. Once that threshold is reached, the estate tax rates are 37% and rise to a hefty 55% for estates of $3 million or more. There's an additional 5% tax on taxable estates between $10 million and $20 million (see Figure 7.1). Estate taxes are typically paid by the estate before bequests are distributed.

MYTH I Must Switch All Accounts into My Own Name

It's not necessary to do this right away. Ultimately, you should change the title and registration of any motor vehicles listed in your husband's name. (You can do that by contacting the Department of Motor Vehicles.) But you only need to do it right away if you plan on selling the car. Likewise, don't rush to remove your husband's name

continues on page 147

FIGURE 7.1   FEDERAL ESTATE TAX RATES

A If Your Taxable Estate Is More Than:	B But Not More Than:	C Then the Tax on the Amount in Column A Is:	D And the Tax Rate on the Excess over the Amounts in Column A Is:
$650,000	$750,000	$211,300	37%
$750,000	$1 million	$248,300	39%
$1 million	$1,250,000	$345,800	41%
$1,250,000	$1,500,000	$448,300	43%
$1,500,000	$2 million	$555,800	45%
$2 million	$2,500,000	$780,000	49%
$2,500,000	$3 million	$1,025,800	53%
$3 million	—	$1,290,800	55%

Each individual is entitled to an *applicable exclusion amount* (the amount that can be transferred during life and at death, estate tax free) (see Figure 7.2). The 1997 Taxpayer Relief Act revised the applicable exclusion amount as follows:

FIGURE 7.2   APPLICABLE EXCLUSION AMOUNT

Year	Applicable Exclusion Amount
1998	$625,000
1999	$650,000
2000–2001	$675,000
2001–2003	$700,000
2004	$850,000
2005	$950,000
2006 and beyond	$1 million

from your telephone listing. A man's name can sometimes help ward off those unsolicited callers who prey on widows. In addition, make sure you change the title of your home, bank account, brokerage accounts, and credit cards.

FACT | You Can Claim a Refund for a Deceased Person

To claim a refund for the tax year in which your husband dies, you'll need to file a separate form. It's called Form 1310, Statement of a Person Claiming Refund Due a Deceased Taxpayer.

If your deceased husband's estate is worth more than the applicable exclusion amount, you must file an estate tax return (form 706). Unlike your regular tax return, this one's not due on April 15, but 9 months after your husband's death. In most cases, you'll have to file a state estate tax or inheritance tax return, too, since states typically follow federal law when it comes to estate taxes. About one-third of the states levy inheritance taxes on funds received by the heirs.

The executor or executrix is responsible for filing these returns, so you'll need to gather the necessary information. In the list that follows, you'll find the documentation needed to file an estate tax return. All of these items won't necessarily apply to your particular situation, and, in many cases, a photocopy rather than the original document will suffice:

- Your husband's will
- His death certificate
- Letters Testamentary (authority from probate court, permitting you, your attorney, or the executor to act)
- His federal and state income tax returns (or your joint tax returns, if you filed jointly) for the 3 years prior to his death
- His federal and state gift tax returns for all years prior to his death
- His bank and brokerage account statements (as well as any joint account statements held with you or someone else) for the 3 years prior to his death

- Any bonds (including savings bonds) and share certificates in which your husband had an interest
- Legal descriptions, such as a deed, and appraisals for any real property (land, a home, an apartment building, etc.) owned individually by your husband or jointly with you or someone else
- Your homeowners' insurance policy(s), including riders for jewelry, art, and other personal property
- Life insurance policy(s); include any policies your husband may have held through his employer
- A list of all assets, such as a car or boat, not included on your insurance policies; also list any jewelry, rare coins, or other items that are stored in your safe deposit box—and that your husband had access to
- Your husband's funeral bills
- A list of his outstanding debts, such as a credit card balance, an auto loan, and/or a doctor or hospital bill
- Promissory notes held by your husband as the lender
- Promissory notes issued by your husband, including charitable pledges
- Your husband's health insurance claims that have not yet been reimbursed
- Trust accounts created by your husband
- Any other trust accounts in which he had a beneficial interest, power of appointment, or trusteeship
- Unpaid claims for tax refunds
- Outstanding mortgages or liens held against any property owned by your husband, or by your husband and you jointly
- Pension or annuity benefits your husband is entitled to, as well as 401(k), 403(b), or 457 plans or Individual Retirement Accounts
- Litigation pending at the time of your husband's death
- Unsatisfied judgments against third parties
- Agreements, financial statements, and income tax returns for your husband's partnership investments for the 5 years prior to his death
- Financial statements and income tax returns for your husband's closely held corporation for the 5 years prior to his death; if your husband's business was family owned, the company's minute book and stock record book for the 5 years prior to his death
- Estimated administration expenses for executors, commissions, legal and accounting fees, court fees, and appraisals

UNDERSTANDING PROBATE

When your husband dies, all of his possessions and finances become part of his estate. The distribution of that estate to beneficiaries such as your children and your husband's favorite charity is then supervised by probate court. (In some states it's called chancery court or surrogate's court.)

Probate is a court-supervised process. During probate, a will is reviewed by the court to make sure it is genuine and legally valid. Probate proves that a will is valid and ensures that the property passes to the people who are supposed to get it. Probate is usually a routine process, but it can take months—even years—to complete, depending upon the complexity of the will, the value of the estate, and the number of beneficiaries.

One disadvantage of the probate process is that once probated, a will is a public document that may be viewed by anyone. Another disadvantage is that passing through probate isn't free. Fees vary from state to state, and are generally based on the fair market value of the assets in the estate. You'll also pay an attorney's fee, and, in many cases, an additional filing fee.

The probate estate isn't simply the value of what your husband owned when he died. Instead, probate assets are those that were owned by your husband alone; all assets your husband owned as a tenant-in-common or as community property; and retirement assets, annuities, and the proceeds of life insurance policies that named the estate—rather than you or another living party—as beneficiary. Generally, if your husband has a probate estate worth more than $60,000, probate is required.

During the probate period, your attorney or the executor will notify the beneficiaries by mail and send each a copy of the will. Your husband's creditors will also be notified, so they can inform the court of any outstanding debts. The necessary papers will be filed in court, and you, the administrator, or the executor should do the following:

- Notify insurance companies, banks, and brokerage firms of your husband's death. Your husband's portion (owner percentage) of the proceeds from all such accounts held as joint tenants-in-common by your husband and other partners, including yourself, must be credited to the estate.
- Take inventory of your husband's assets. That means everything, including your spouse's 401(k) plan; IRA; pension; stocks and bonds; life insurance policies (include only those owned by him; do not

include those owned by a trust or by you); checking, savings, and/or money market accounts; car; house; and business. If you owned assets jointly, these assets may not pass through probate, depending upon the laws of the state in which you live.

- Value your assets. For assets with hard-to-determine values, such as antiques, collectibles, or a business, you'll need an appraisal. Generally, assets are valued by determining a fair-market equivalent (you can look in the *Kelley Blue Book* (www.kbb.com) to find out how much your husband's prized Mercedes convertible is worth) or by hiring a certified appraiser (check the Yellow Pages, ask friends, or contact the American Society of Appraisers at 800-272-8258).
- List your husband's liabilities. Include all of his outstanding debts, such as the balances on his credit cards and the bills for his car phone and online computer service. Recording these liabilities correctly could reduce his taxable estate.
- Open a checking account for the estate. Deposit all cash holdings and any monies due your husband in the future. Funeral expenses, attorney fees, taxes, and other expenses can be paid from this account. To set up such an account, you'll need a taxpayer identification number for the estate. (Call 800-829-3676 to get the IRS's Form SS-4.)

Once the debts of the estate are paid, the estate is distributed according to the terms of the will, or by state law if there is no will. Your attorney or the executor then notifies the court that probate has been completed.

If your husband didn't have a will—and a surprising number of people do not—you must go through a process of *administration* instead. In this situation an administrator is appointed to settle the estate. The process, however, is much like probate.

To avoid the probate process entirely, your husband must have passed his property to beneficiaries outside of a will. He could have accomplished this in three basic ways. Perhaps all of your husband's assets were in trusts. (Generally, trusts pass outside of the estate and avoid probate.) Similarly, assets that were held jointly by you and your husband—called *joint tenancy with rights of survivorship*—are generally transferred directly to you, the deceased's spouse, without going through probate court. The proceeds of a life insurance policy, an annuity, or retirement assets like a 401(k) plan that name you or someone else as a beneficiary don't pass through probate either. (If your husband's life insurance was payable to his estate—and not you directly—the proceeds will be probated.)

When You Can't Find Needed Documents

You're fortunate if your husband kept good financial records. But those documents may not be on hand when you need them. Most people's financial papers, it seems, are stored in a number of places.

The most likely hiding spot? Your husband's safe deposit box. Generally, this box is sealed once the bank learns of your husband's death. (Joint safe deposit boxes are sealed sometimes, too.) To unseal the box, you must obtain an Application for Release from your state department of taxation. (The address and phone number should be listed in the phone book under *State Agencies*.) Either your attorney or the estate's executor needs authorization from the probate court (commonly called Letters Testamentary, Letters of Administration, or a Certificate of Letters) to open the box. The executor then takes these papers to the bank or financial institution that houses the safe deposit box and asks that the box be opened. This is a good reason *not* to keep your wills in a safe deposit box, as you'll want the document immediately.

If the documents aren't in the safe deposit box after all—or if you can't find the safe deposit box—you'll have to do some sleuthing. Check out the places your husband kept his papers. Review his checkbook, credit card receipts, bank statements, and canceled checks. These documents should tell you about what he owned—and what he owed. Ask permission to check his desk at work for personal records. Don't forget to look in his briefcase, dresser drawers, and even his wallet.

For a birth or marriage certificate, call the County Clerk's office in the county where the birth or marriage took place. They'll supply a certified copy if you can't find the originals. For a duplicate Social Security card, call Social Security (800-772-1213).

CASH FLOW MANAGEMENT

Once your husband's estate is closed—and the assets have been distributed—you should start thinking about your finances. How much money do you have? What are your monthly expenses? Do you need more insurance? Are you saving enough for retirement?

Many women, especially those who were raised in traditional households, don't know where to begin. While they may have handled the weekly household budget, these wives often left the family's financial planning largely to their husbands. Now, managing the family's finances is a black hole that they somehow must approach.

When Elsie, a 74-year-old woman, came to my office a few years ago, she was very uncomfortable with financial matters. Her husband of 52 years—who had handled every aspect of the couple's finances—had just died. Elsie was paralyzed to take the next step. She didn't know how to read her bank statement or make out a withdrawal slip. I soon realized that Elsie didn't need financial planning per se but an understanding of basic money concepts. So we studied her bank and brokerage statements line by line. I showed her how to use an ATM.

If you're as money-averse as Elsie, you probably should see a financial planner to help get your finances organized. (See Chapter 11 for advice on picking a financial planner.) But most women—even those with no experience managing money—can get a handle on their finances. Where to start? Think about where you want to go and how you might get there. In other words, define your goals. You must think short, medium, and long term. (Depending on your situation, short-term goals are up to 3 years from now, mid-term about 3 to 7 years, and long-term about 7 years or more.) It's important to break goals down this way because your saving and investment strategies will differ depending on your time frame.

Your life has already changed so much since your husband died that it can be frightening to look into the future and plan a life without him. But you must. (That's what this book is all about, in fact.) Think about your priorities. They may be as basic as putting dinner on the table and keeping your home without going into debt. Or they could be as sophisticated as designing a charitable trust to benefit your favorite organization or in your husband's memory.

To turn those goals into reality, you need to calculate two figures: your net worth and your cash flow. Net worth is simply your assets (what you own) minus your liabilities (what you owe). This number should be relatively easy to figure because you already have your husband's net worth (as a result of the probate proceedings). Simply take the portion of his net worth figure that you inherited, add any assets that you own by yourself, and voila—you have your net worth (see Figure 7.3).

Cash flow, on the other hand, is your income minus your expenses. Often, this is a tougher calculation. Most people don't know where their money goes. In fact, when I ask clients how much money they spend,

---

FIGURE 7.3 NET WORTH WORKSHEET

Your Net Worth As of _____

Assets

Cash equivalents

Checking accounts	$_____
Savings accounts	_____
Money market accounts	_____
Money market fund accounts	_____
Certificates of deposit	_____
U.S. Treasury bills	_____
Cash value of life insurance	_____
Total	$_____

Investments

Stocks	_____
Bonds	_____
Mutual fund investments	_____
Partnership interests	_____
Other investments	_____
Total	$_____

Retirement funds

Pension (present lump-sum value)	_____
IRAs and Keogh accounts	_____

continues

FIGURE 7.3   NET WORTH WORKSHEET (CONTINUED)

Employee savings plans
(e.g., 401(k), SEP, ESOP)   _____
   Total $_____

Personal assets
  Principal residence   _____
  Second residence   _____
  Collectibles/art/antiques   _____
  Automobiles   _____
  Home furnishings   _____
  Other assets   _____
   Total $_____
  Total assets $_____

Liabilities
  Charge account balances   _____
  Personal loans   _____
  Student loans   _____
  Auto loans   _____
  401(k) loans   _____
  Investment loans (margin,
   real estate, etc.)   _____
  Home mortgages   _____
  Home equity loans   _____
  Alimony   _____
  Child support   _____
  Life insurance policy loans   _____
  Projected income tax
   liability   _____
  Other liabilities   _____
  Total liabilities $(_____)

  Net worth (assets
   minus liabilities) $_____

their financial profile generally looks great on paper: their income clearly exceeds their expenses. But then real life intervenes—you buy that cup of coffee and danish every morning on the way to work or you shop the sales on your lunch hour—and those neat little columns of figures quickly disappear.

For your purposes right now, you need to know how much it's costing you to live each month. To get an accurate picture, some women find they must write down every expenditure (yes, even that 75 cents for the newspaper) in a small notebook for a month or so. Others simply use their checkbooks as a guide. If you're comfortable with a computer, you can use some simple software to help you, or use our worksheet (see Chapter 1) as a model if you prefer pencil and paper.

Next, you need to see if your current income will cover your expenses in the future. You've no doubt read that inflation can erode your buying power. It's true. Even if inflation stays as low as it is today (about 2%), in 20 years you'll need $148 to buy what $100 buys today. Unfortunately, you probably won't be able to calculate this future income question by yourself. A financial planner can help you, or, if you have a computer, you can buy a program like Ernst & Young's *Prosper*® to do the math for you. (The inflation calculations above, for instance, were done using *Prosper*.)

Whatever the numbers ultimately reveal, you need to manage what you have in the best way possible (known as asset management). Here's where that net worth number comes into play. How much of that net worth (which you calculated above) is available for investing? What are you going to do with the proceeds from your husband's life insurance policy, for example? The lump-sum pension fund distribution from his job? His annuity? Whatever investment vehicle your money is in—stocks, bonds, mutual funds, Treasury bills, or real estate, to name a few—you have to make sure it fits into your financial game plan. If you need to earn 10% on that money for the next 10 years to keep pace with inflation, for example, then you probably should forgo conservative investments like certificates of deposit and think about something riskier, such as stocks, that offer higher returns.

Not surprisingly, widows are generally reluctant to change their husbands' investments—even if those investments aren't financially sound. I recently worked with a 70-year-old woman who had been widowed for 10 years. Sarah's husband had left her a substantial portfolio, which she had let stand as it was. Most of that money was invested in limited partnerships—all the rage a dozen years ago. Unfortunately, many limited partnerships did not live up to expectations and are now worth only a small percentage of the original investment. Sarah had the partnerships listed at what they had cost to purchase. After a bit of research, we soon discovered that these partnerships she'd clung to for 10 years had actually decreased in value by more than 80%.

Ironically, Sarah was a much more successful investor on her own. After her husband died, she boned up on investment basics from books and magazines and invested the money from her part-time job as a saleswoman in a variety of stock and bond mutual funds. I didn't have to reallocate her assets at all. She simply needed me to confirm that she was doing fine—money-wise—on her own. And that's a lesson all women, but especially widows, should take to heart: Have faith in yourself. Even if your husband was the financial brains in your marriage, you can—with time—understand and manage your bank statements, credit cards, stocks, bonds, trusts, and other investments. Like Sarah, you may be surprisingly good at managing this thing called money.

Your E&Y Planner Says:

Oftentimes, the biggest mistake widows can make is to pay off the mortgage with the life insurance proceeds. Although it's emotionally tempting to live mortgage free, that's not necessarily your best move financially. Too often, I've seen widows with paid-off houses scrambling to pay the electric bill at the end of the month. You need some of your assets to be liquid. How much? The general rule of thumb is that you need 3 to 6 months of daily living expenses tucked away in an emergency cash reserve fund. But if you plan on supplementing your income over the next few years with the proceeds of your husband's estate, you should probably keep more cash on hand.

If you are considering paying off the mortgage, you need to compare the cost of your mortgage and cash outlay per month to the income you are earning on the proceeds from the estate to decide the best course of action.

FACT **Women Outlive Men by 7 Years**

Unfortunately, many women not only outlive their husbands, but their husbands' retirement income as well. Before 1984, a widow might have lost access to her spouse's pension when he died. Today, thanks to the Retirement Equity Act of 1984, widows now have some protection. Private pension plans will pay survivor benefits to widows—typically 50% of the benefit paid while the husband was alive—unless the women waive this protection in writing beforehand.

LOOKING AHEAD:
What You Should Be Doing Right Now

No one likes to think about widowhood, much less prepare for it. But when your husband or life partner dies, the last thing you need is a lot of unanswered questions. Did he have a will? Where's the safe deposit box key? How much can you expect from his pension? Instead, spend some time now—no matter what your age or how long you've been married—and get the following financial information in order:

- *The will.* Does your husband have one? Where is it stored?
- *The safe deposit box.* If your husband has one, make sure you know where the key is and what the box contains.
- *Bank accounts and other investments.* Keep a list handy of all your accounts: those held separately and those held jointly.
- *Debts.* How much do you owe, and to whom?
- *Documents.* Know where his birth certificate and Social Security card are, as well as the deed to the house and his life insurance policies. Get the facts on your homeowners', auto, and medical insurance.
- *The pension.* How much can you expect to receive? Whom do you contact at his former employer to get payment sent to you?

- *Professionals.* List the names, addresses, and telephone numbers of the family's lawyer, financial planner, stockbroker, and accountant.
- *Funeral plans.* It is morbid and painful, so take care of your own and your spouse's funeral arrangements. Buying a cemetery plot and knowing what arrangements you want—and how much they will cost—ahead of time can make a difficult period a little easier.

8

WIDOWHOOD: SPECIAL ISSUES

No one likes to think about the death of a loved one. The possibility of losing your husband can seem so overwhelming, in fact, that many women simply choose never to think about it. They put off drawing up a will, discussing estate planning, even talking about how much life insurance is needed. When death does strike, it can be one of the most traumatic experiences of your life. And, unfortunately, it can strike even when you are quite young. If you haven't taken any steps to prepare yourself ahead of time, your world will become that much more chaotic when you are widowed.

As is true at other milestones in your life, the death of your husband raises new financial concerns that must be addressed. In the last chapter we talked about the general steps every widow must take to get her financial life in order. Unfortunately, many of these issues must be handled by you—and shortly after your husband's death.

Once the proper papers are filed, however, a widow's path may follow any number of routes. Some widows will continue to live much the same lives they did before their husbands died. Other widows' lives will change more dramatically because they must return to paid employment, sell the family home and move to smaller quarters, and/or dip into their savings to maintain their standard of living. Still others may find themselves in more dire straits, especially if their husbands didn't leave a sizable insurance policy, a pension, or some other savings plan.

Your age at the time of widowhood will naturally play a significant role. A 75-year-old widow may worry if she can support herself through her old age, for example, and if she has enough medical insurance. A 30-something widow with two young children, on the other hand, will worry about saving for her own retirement and sending the kids to college. To understand the various issues that women may face at this critical juncture in their lives, let's take a close look at a few women who have experienced widowhood.

THE YOUNG WIDOW

Dana, the mother of Courtney, age 10, and Joe, age 5, was widowed at age 35. She hadn't worked since her first child was born 10 years before. Although her husband—the sole family breadwinner—had recently died, Dana wanted to remain at home with her children for the next several years. She didn't want to return to paid work until the youngest had finished elementary school. Could she do that?

Her husband's insurance policy had paid her $350,000 and was currently sitting in a bank money market account. It was yielding an after-tax return of 2%. In addition, Dana was entitled to Social Security benefits totaling $1,500 for herself as a surviving spouse caring for dependent children under age 16 and for her children. Her late husband had a 401(k) plan worth $150,000 and she had an IRA worth $10,000. The couple also owned a home with an outstanding mortgage of $100,000.

After analyzing Dana's cash flow, it appeared that her money fell short. She couldn't stay at home full time, send the kids to private college, *and* leave her retirement nest egg untouched. It was time to make some tough choices. I outlined her options for her. She could:

1. *Invest more aggressively.* Her oldest child wouldn't be starting college for another 8 years; the youngest, 13 years. Because she had so much time to allow her money to grow, Dana could invest a portion of her husband's life insurance settlement in equities rather than the con-

servative money market account it was currently placed in. Over time, many stocks and stock mutual funds (commonly referred to as equities) have had average annual returns of 11% or more.

2. *Go back to work sooner.* That would bring additional money in.

3. *Sell the house and buy a smaller home with no mortgage.* Her monthly expenses could be cut substantially.

4. *Pick a less expensive college.* By the year 2010, it's estimated that the annual cost of her child's college education will be $60,341 at an Ivy League school, $41,484 at an out-of-state university, and $22,628 at a state university.

5. *Use part of her retirement money to fund the children's college education.*

What did Dana do? I strongly discouraged her from dipping into her retirement money. In general, it's not a smart idea to risk your own future so that your children can attend an expensive college. Dana didn't want to sell her house because she was concerned about upsetting the children. They needed stability at this point in their lives.

Dana did invest her assets more aggressively, keeping 25% in cash and distributing the rest among a mix of stock and bond funds. This was a combination she felt comfortable with. She also planned to return to work in 5 years instead of 9. If money remained tight, she would consider public college rather than private school for the children. I also advised her that scholarships might be available for her children, depending on her financial position at the time.

Once we had settled Dana's cash flow problems, we needed to address some other estate planning issues. First, Dana had to draft a new will now that she was a single parent. She needed to name a guardian for her children and decided on her sister, Carly. But she was worried that Carly, a woman of modest means, wouldn't be able to provide for the children financially—even with the estate the children would inherit from Dana.

We did some more calculating and determined that a $500,000 life insurance policy for Dana—naming Carly as the beneficiary—would give Carly enough money to raise the children. You can deal with life insurance in a number of ways, such as putting the policy in trust, for example. But in this case, it seemed simpler for Carly to purchase and hold a $500,000 term policy on Dana's life. Since Dana was young, healthy, and a non-smoker, Carly bought a 15-year level term policy for just $500 per year. The premium is fairly low and the policy will be in effect until both children are expected to finish college. Also, structuring the insurance that way, the payout—should Dana die—would not go through her estate. Nor would it go to the children. Instead, the money would go directly to Carly, who, Dana felt, would be better able to make judgments about how the funds should be spent. However, if she doesn't use a trust, she is trusting her sister to use the money for her children.

Second, Dana wanted to make sure her husband's retirement assets were allocated correctly. His 401(k) plan, invested entirely in the stock of her husband's company, badly needed diversification. We decided to roll the retirement fund into an IRA immediately and allocated the funds as follows: 65% in stock mutual funds (including international funds) and 35% in bond mutual funds (including international funds). Given Dana's age, goals, time horizon, and risk tolerance, this was an asset allocation she felt comfortable with.

And that's the end of the story—for now. Dana and I still meet periodically to update her financial plan and discuss any problems that may arise.

Some additional issues that Dana—and other young widows— might be concerned about include the following:

Job Retraining

Women (more so than men) tend to shape their lives to fit their families. So when the family structure changes after the death of a husband, a woman's career often changes, too. This isn't easy, especially if you've been home raising a family and now must gain paid employment outside the home.

If you don't have a degree, consider getting one. If funds are low, you can attend classes part time at a public college. While it's possible to land a job without a bachelor's degree, it's tough to find a position that pays well and is challenging—especially if you're more than 35 years old. You might also consider getting some technical training in computer skills or the sciences. If you've been out of the workforce for a while and want to return to the type of work you did before, take a refresher course or join an association in your field. Professional organizations often provide courses, and they're a great place to network for a job.

Don't forget to scan the want ads. It's free, and you just might find some job possibilities or leads for other jobs. Read the requirements carefully, and write a letter and resume to fit each job description. Include any volunteer work if it relates to the job in some way. Consider getting help from a trained job counselor to put together your resume. Also, network with friends, relatives, and neighbors for possible referrals

Retirement Savings

If your husband had a self-directed retirement plan, such as a 401(k), 403(b), Keogh, SEP, or IRA, you may have decisions to make. Depending on your current age and his age at death, you may want to roll this plan over into your own IRA or a new IRA. If the IRA is in your name, you don't have to take distributions until you reach age 70½ (although you can start anytime after age 59½). If you put the IRA in you husband's name instead, you have to start taking the money out in the year when he would have reached age 70½.

An advantage of keeping the IRA in your husband's name is that, as the beneficiary, you can take money out at any age (even before age 59½) without having to pay a 10% early withdrawal tax. So if you need to use some of this money to cover your living expenses, this may be the best choice for you. However, if you don't need the money before 59½ anyway, and especially if your husband was quite a bit older than you, then putting the IRA in your name will allow you to wait longer until distributions are required; the IRA funds could build up to much more than if you took the money out earlier and paid income taxes on it sooner.

You should also think about your own retirement plan. Now's the time to contribute as much as you can to a 401(k) plan, for instance, especially if your employer matches your contribution. You must also change the beneficiary on your own retirement account if your husband had previously been named.

Depending on your income level, you should also consider putting money into a Roth IRA, a new retirement savings vehicle. You can invest $2,000 in a Roth IRA per year if your adjusted gross income (AGI) is less than $95,000 (for 1998) as a single taxpayer. The contribution is nondeductible for taxes, but the money grows tax-deferred and the earnings are never subject to income taxes.

Raising the Children

Many young widows don't realize how dramatically their financial picture will change with the absence of their husband's salary. At this time, it's crucial that you look ahead and determine, like Dana, what expenses you can expect to have and how you'll pay for them. In most cases, it will be necessary to modify your spending patterns. Many young widows find this process daunting, even depressing. But it's important to remember that this new financial situation is not permanent. Your current expenses, such as day care for the children if necessary, will decrease over time. Your salary, meanwhile, will probably increase (because you're returning to work after a long hiatus or you're simply moving up in your career).

Income Tax Planning

In general, the same basic income tax rules apply after one spouse's death as when both are living. For example, IRA distributions that were taxable during your husband's life will also be taxable to you, the beneficiary, when you take money out of your husband's IRA. One important difference is the tax on capital gains. Capital assets like stocks and real estate, including your home, receive what is called a "stepped-up basis" if they are included in your husband's estate (that is, if they were in his name). This basically means that you can sell these assets and not pay any tax on the gain that was there as of the date of his death. (If these assets were held jointly, then ½ of their value receives a stepped-up basis.) So, you can feel free to sell these assets and either reinvest the money or spend it without having to pay any tax on capital gain.

Applying for Social Security Benefits

Under current rules, you can receive widows' benefits if you are age 60 or older. However, you can claim a widow's benefit at any age if you have dependent children who are under the age of 16 or disabled living with you. Your unmarried children may also receive survivors' benefits on your husband's record until they are age 18 (or age 19 if they are attending school full time). A disabled child can continue to receive benefits after age 18 and may even qualify for supplemental security income disability benefits.

The amount of your monthly payment will depend on your age when you start getting benefits and on the amount your deceased husband would have been entitled to, or was receiving, when he died. Social Security also establishes a maximum family benefit that you and your children may receive. As a widow, you should receive:

- 100% if you are normal retirement age (currently 65 or older)
- 71.5% or greater depending on your age if you are between 60 and normal retirement age

To apply, you'll probably need the following documents: both your husband's and your own Social Security numbers, your birth certificate, your marriage certificate, your husband's death certificate, your divorce papers if you're applying as a surviving divorced spouse, your children's Social Security numbers, and the name of your bank and the account number so your benefits can be directly deposited into your account.

If you aren't already getting Social Security benefits, you should apply for widows' benefits promptly. In some cases, benefits are not retroactive. You can apply by phone, online, or at any Social Security office.

If you're already getting Social Security benefits as a wife on your husband's record, you should report the death to Social Security. They'll analyze your situation to determine if you will receive higher payments from widows' benefits. If you're getting benefits on your own record, you must complete an application to get widows' benefits. As a widow, you can generally receive the greater of your husband's Social Security payments or your Social Security payments. So, often your benefits will increase.

Updating Your Own Insurance

Without the benefit of a second income to fall back on, you probably need additional life and disability insurance, which will pay benefits if you die or if you're unable to work. How much insurance you need depends on how many children you have and how old they are. You may be able to get coverage through your employer or a trade association. If that's not enough, or if you cannot obtain such coverage, you'll have to buy your own policy through an insurance broker.

THE OLDER WIDOW

Sophie, age 60, was looking forward to retirement. She had been working as an administrative assistant for the past 10 years, but now that her husband had recently passed away, she wanted to spend time with her four grandchildren, travel, and just relax a bit. She was confident in her plans.

Sophie's cash flow and net worth told a different story, however. Aside from her house, car, furniture, and personal belongings, Sophie's only asset was a $20,000 savings account, which was all that remained of the $100,000 insurance proceeds she had received when her husband died. Sophie had used three-quarters of the proceeds to pay off her mortgage, and she'd been using the remaining money to supplement her small salary. Neither she nor her husband had set up any kind of a retirement fund.

Her net worth looked bad, but her cash flow was worse. I asked Sophie to keep track of her expenses for a month. We soon discovered that she was spending $450 a month more than her take-home pay! That explained the drain on her savings account. Sophie was shocked and saddened. Would she wind up like so many widows she'd heard about, living in poverty?

Not necessarily. It was time to take an ax to her budget. The first thing to go was the $700 she was spending every month for food. Sophie was eating out every night because she hated cooking for herself. I asked Sophie how many other widows lived nearby. Ten, she said, and none of them enjoyed eating alone. So Sophie started The Supper Club. Every Tuesday and Thursday night the club members take turns cooking meals for each other. That inspired Sophie to stop eating out so much on other nights, and even to take her lunch to work. The result? Sophie's food budget dropped from $700 per month to $200.

And that's what we did to nearly every category in her budget. Obviously the fixed expenses like heat and water remained constant, but Sophie cut back on everything from clothing to toys for her grandkids to prescription drugs. (The latter resulted from a carefully researched switch to an HMO from a traditional indemnity plan.) Sophie also began contributing to her company's health care spending account so that she paid for some of her medical expenses with pre-tax dollars.

While Sophie isn't out of the woods yet, she's well on her way to living within her means. She knows she'll have to work until she's at least age 70, and that even then money will be tight. But she now knows what she needs to do, and that gives her hope.

Some additional issues that Sophie—and other older widows—may be concerned about include the following:

Applying for Social Security Benefits

You may begin taking reduced Social Security benefits based on your own earnings at age 62, or standard benefits at the normal retirement age (see Figure 10.3 in Chapter 10.) If you are entitled to retirement benefits on your own work record, you can take reduced retirement payments at age 62 and then receive the full widow's benefit at age 65, or you can take reduced widows' benefits until normal retirement age and then file a claim for full retirement benefits on your own record.

The longer you wait to receive your benefits, however, the higher the amount will be. If you delay your retirement beyond the normal retirement age your future benefits will increase each year by a certain percentage. If you were born in 1935, for example, your benefit will increase 6% each year you delay retirement between ages 65 and 70. You can defer receiving benefits until age 70. If you are under age 70 and continue working, you will receive reduced benefits if your earnings exceed a certain amount.

Additionally, if you choose to remarry after the age of 60, you can still generally receive Social Security benefits from your deceased spouse's record.

Pensions and Other Retirement Savings

Your husband may have had a defined pension plan (through his employer) that continues to pay you a monthly pension after his death. In the past, the surviving spouse received 50% of this benefit. Now, depending on the pension and the payment options available to your husband, the surviving spouse could receive up to 100% of the pension benefit. If your husband had not retired, you may be able to choose how you'd like the money distributed (i.e., as a lump sum or an annuity).

If your husband had a pension or profit sharing plan at his employer, you may have a choice how you take the money—for example, a lump-sum distribution or a monthly annuity for life. The advantages of taking a lump sum include receiving your money all at once and having complete control over how to invest it. Some advantages of an annuity are that it provides a regular stream of income that you cannot outlive, and that you don't have to worry about investing it. If you have this choice, you should consult a tax adviser for assistance because the situation can be complicated and you want to make sure you understand the results of your choices.

If your husband was already receiving an annuity from a pension plan, the payments will continue to you if it's a joint and survivor annuity, but the amount you get each month may be less than what your husband was receiving, depending on what type of annuity it is.

Updating Your Health Insurance Coverage

If your husband worked for a company that has a health plan covering 20 or more employees, under the terms of the federal Consolidated Omnibus Reconciliation Act (COBRA) law, the plan must continue to offer you coverage for 36 months. You must pay the premiums, however. If you are 65 or older, you're eligible for Medicare. Medicare has two parts. There is no premium or fee for Part A, which covers hospital services. Medicare Part A can also help pay for inpatient hospital care, inpatient care in a skilled nursing facility, home health care, and hospice care. Part A is financed during your working years through the FICA tax.

Medicare Part B pays for coverage of your doctor's bills and many other medical services and supplies that aren't covered by Medicare Part A. (Prescription drugs are not covered, however.) Part B is optional and is offered when you become entitled to Part A. If you do not want Part B, you must elect not to take it. There is a monthly premium and you will be billed unless you decline coverage. Together, Medicare Parts A and B don't cover every medical need. That's why many older consumers buy a supplemental Medigap policy. (For a more detailed discussion of Medigap polices, see Chapter 10.)

As an older widow you also need to prepare your estate and think about long-term care should you become ill. (See Chapter 5 for information on long-term care policies.) If your finances get tight, here are some practical financial steps to consider:

- Share your home and its expenses with a friend or relative.
- If you have a larger home with high maintenance, move to a smaller home that is easier to care for.
- Work part time in retirement (see Chapter 10).
- Stay in your current home and take out a reverse mortgage (see Chapter 5 for this option).
- Consider moving in with one of your children.
- Make sure you have uncovered all of your husband's assets. Search his papers and file cabinets for forgotten life insurance policies, bank accounts, etc. Contact his former employers to see if you are entitled to any payments from their pension plans.
- If you need extra cash, you should generally use up your cash and other investments before you take money out of an IRA or retirement plan. This is because you will have to pay income tax on those withdrawals, so in order to end up with an additional $1,000 to spend, you may have to take out $1,500 from an IRA to cover the income taxes as well. Of course, the amount of the tax due depends on your own income tax bracket.

9

THE ENTREPRENEURIAL LIFE

For many people, owning your own business is still the American Dream. No boss. No corporate rat race. Control over your own destiny. And a fortune to be made if you do it right. After all, what is a successful entrepreneur but an individual with a dream—who had the tenacity and the smarts to turn that dream into a business reality?

Of course, a great idea is not enough to launch a successful business. If you have considered starting your own business, you have many options from which to choose. You can take your own idea, obtain funding, organize a company, and seek success on your own. You can buy someone else's existing business and run it yourself. You can purchase a franchise with a recognizable product, existing supply network, and uniform business procedures. You can even become an independent consultant and work from your home. No matter which route you take, however, you need to proceed carefully and consider all aspects of the situation before you commit yourself.

ARE YOU THE ENTREPRENEURIAL TYPE?

You may have a strong inclination toward going into business for yourself, but it's not a way of life that suits everyone. One of the most important factors in building a successful business is probably the willingness to work hard. (Some people call it self-discipline.) Most entrepreneurs work harder than they did when employed by someone else. One reason is that they themselves are in charge now; another is that they're more driven than they were when following someone else's game plan. As an entrepreneur setting up a new business, you can generally expect to work 6 or 7 days a week, 10 to 15 hours per day, for the first few years. Not everyone is ready to work this hard, of course, but it's almost impossible to find a successful business person who hasn't done so (at least initially).

 When You Run Your Own Business, You Don't Have to Answer to a Boss. You're Completely Autonomous.

As the owner of a small business, you may not answer to a boss per se, but you must still answer to your clients or customers—many of whom may be at least as demanding as a boss.

Then there are the sacrifices. Loss of an income is usually the first—and most painful—sacrifice you'll make as an entrepreneur. Unless you have a substantial contingency fund to cover your expenses during this early start-up period, you will probably have to cut your spending and possibly incur some debt. (Many people have a contingency fund to cover 6 months' worth of living expenses. But your business may not provide you with an income for several years or more.)

As an entrepreneur launching a new business, you'll probably also have to forfeit time to get the business off the ground—time otherwise spent with your spouse or family, or pursuing hobbies or other interests. You may even postpone getting married and starting a family. And when your friends call to invite you to spend the weekend playing tennis or vacationing, you will stay at home or go to the office to tend to your business.

 Your E&Y Planner Says:

You won't have to make sacrifices forever if your business is a success. As the owner of your own business, you have the potential to reap wealth and fame. But that's down the road. If you're going to succeed, you must be prepared to say no to many of life's pleasures during the infancy of your business venture.

How can you find out whether you have what it takes to make it as an entrepreneur? There are firms that offer assistance to people making the transition from the corporate world to self-employment. These companies provide testing, counseling, and planning that can help you determine if the entrepreneurial life is right for you. Or, you can think about the statements listed in Figure 9.1. These statements are reasons people often cite for going into business for themselves; they may help you clarify your reasons for becoming an entrepreneur.

FIGURE 9.1   EVALUATING WHY ENTREPRENEURSHIP INTERESTS YOU
There are no right or wrong statements. Review this checklist and mark the statements that express your interest in entrepreneurship. Prioritize them from the most important to the least.

_____ You prefer to be your own boss.

_____ You feel dissatisfied in a corporate environment.

_____ You've determined that your opportunities for advancement are limited in your current position.

_____ You have a business idea you want to explore.

_____ You want to change your goals.

_____ You're tired of hunting for jobs in the marketplace.

_____ You want to take advantage of an opportunity that has arisen.

_____ You want to avoid relocating to another geographical area to pursue your current occupation.

_____ You need to express your creativity.

_____ You believe you can make more money by running your own company.

_____ You need employment that's more personally satisfying.

_____ You want to make good use of a financial windfall.

_____ You want to see if you can succeed on your own.

CONSIDER YOUR OPTIONS

To go into business for yourself, you have four basic options:

- Starting your own business
- Buying or investing in an existing business
- Buying a franchise
- Becoming an independent consultant

Starting Your Own Business

Starting your own business commonly means producing and selling a product or service. This can include a variety of ventures, from manufacturing widgets to selling ice cream at the local mall. The advantage of running your own business is that you're your own boss and you keep the fruits of your labor (assuming the business is successful, of course). In addition, you get to take your idea from conception to completion, which for many entrepreneurs is extremely satisfying. The drawbacks are that you bear the full responsibility of the operation's success or failure and that you may have a reduced cash flow for an extended period of time. Also, most new business owners don't have a support system to rely on. They learn how to run the business on the job.

Buying an Existing Business

If you like the idea of running your own business but want to circumvent the start-up stage, you can consider buying an existing business that has an established customer base, a network of suppliers and distributors, and a history of profits. The advantages to this arrangement are that you can earn a salary from the very beginning through the business's ongoing cash flow and that the seller of the business should be able to provide some training and possibly even financing. The drawbacks are that you won't be creating your own business from scratch and the business may grow at a slower rate than a brand-new venture.

Buying a Franchise

When you buy a franchise, you are both the boss and an employee. On the one hand, you own and run your franchised outlet, which can be anything from a housecleaning service to a fast-food restaurant. On the other hand, however, you must follow the system and the rules of the franchisor who owns the concept. In exchange for the franchisor's support, expertise, and established reputation, you pay a percentage of your sales. The advantages to buying a franchise are that you're using a recognized name, trademark, and business appearance as well as gaining the benefits of the franchisor's previous track record. The downside is that your flexibility is limited and the franchisor may have exaggerated the firm's success.

Becoming an Independent Consultant

Independent consultants play a wide variety of roles within the corporate world as well as the legal, medical, academic, and political spheres. Given the trend of corporate downsizing and hiring of nonstaff contractors, it seems likely that an increasing number of people will work as consultants. One advantage of being a consultant is that you limit your capital investment and overhead expenses. You also have the potential for high annual income and a flexible work schedule. The drawbacks are that you lack a built-in support system and you must compete with a large number of other consultants to win a contract or assignment. Cash flow is generally irregular, too.

A CASE STUDY: REFINE YOUR DREAM

Sara has always loved to cook, so she was very excited when she learned that the owner of her favorite gourmet food and kitchen shop wanted to sell the business. Sara had been working as an administrative assistant in the same company for years. To Sara, this was an uninteresting, repetitive job that helped her pay the bills. But the gourmet food shop? It could be her chance to run her own business!

Sara did some quick calculations. She had enough money in the bank to support herself for 1 year, but that would leave nothing for a down payment on the store. Her parents were already retired and living on a fixed income, so they probably couldn't lend her more than a small sum. Sara expected a substantial bonus at year end from her employer, but that was 3 months away. Unfortunately, Sara soon realized that she couldn't afford to buy the store.

That didn't dissuade Sara from pursuing her dream of entrepreneurship. Over the next 12 months, she began saving as much money as possible—and boning up on how to start a business. She took a bookkeeping course at the local community college as well as a class that taught her the essentials of entrepreneurship. Sara visited a variety of food and kitchen supply stores in the area, noting their display and marketing concepts, their customer traffic flow, and the types of product sold. She even mapped out a business plan.

That's when the idea struck her. She was trying to do too much too soon. She couldn't sell both gourmet food *and* gourmet kitchenware, at least not right away. So Sara quickly scaled down her dream: She'd open up just a gourmet kitchenware shop. The food aspect would wait until she was more established. Kitchen facilities were too expensive for the start-up phase of her business.

Shortly thereafter, Sara began looking for commercial space and an accountant. Her sister, a commercial artist, offered to design a logo and letterhead for her as a Christmas present. The last I heard from her, Sara was negotiating a loan with her local bank.

CREATING A BUSINESS PLAN

To build your business you need a road map, or *business plan.* Although the contents and lengths of these documents vary according to the business they plan, every start-up venture needs a business plan. Why? First, a business plan helps you develop ideas about how you should conduct your business. It's a chance to refine your strategies. A good business plan will take a hard look, for instance, at the geographic area and/or neighborhood in which you want to operate your business: Certain businesses may not do well in a particular area. Second, it's a tool you can use to assess your company's performance over time. You can use the financial part of a business plan, for example, as the basis for an operating budget. Third, a good business plan will help you raise capital. To raise money for your company, you must prepare a detailed plan and then let potential lenders or investors review it.

> **Your E&Y Planner Says:**
>
> A business plan that's going to be used solely to help you manage the business may not need to be as in depth as one that's intended to attract investors or secure a loan.

Business plans follow a standardized formal structure that reviewers will expect in any document you submit. You should divide your business plan into sections, not chapters. Here's the standard sequence and a brief description of what each section contains:

Table of contents. This serves the same function as a table of contents for a book.

Executive summary. This is a summary of the entire plan.

General company description. In this brief section, you should indicate the type of business you're proposing (manufacturer, retailer, or service business), your expected customer base, your location, and your business objectives.

Products and services. You must describe your product or service. Supply a physical description (if applicable) and the product's stage of development.

Marketing plan. This is one of the most important parts of the business plan. It explains how you expect to generate sales. You must define the market, your competition, and your market strategy.

Operational plan. This section addresses how your business will create its product and services.

Management and organization. A few questions that you should address include: Will management be participative or autocratic? Will responsibilities and tasks be sharply defined?

Management team/principals. You must discuss the backgrounds of your company's key players, such as yourself (the entrepreneur), investors, and members of the board of directors.

Organizational chart. You need to explain the relationships and divisions of responsibility within the organization.

Policy and strategy. You should also include an explanation of how employees will be selected, trained, and rewarded.

Structure and capitalization. Here's where you identify what legal form you'll use (i.e., partnership or a corporation) and how you'll capitalize the venture.

Financial plan. This is a comprehensive set of projections that reflect your company's anticipated financial performance. When do you expect the company to become profitable, for instance? What will the first year's expenses be? What's your projected cash flow?

ORGANIZING YOUR BUSINESS

You must choose the legal form under which your business will operate. The three major variables you must deal with when choosing the legal form of your business are liability, control, and taxes. To determine the type of structure that best suits your needs, ask yourself the following questions:

- Will you be the sole owner? If not, how much control will each owner have?
- Are you willing to be personally liable for any debts or claims made against the business?
- Which form of business offers the most tax advantages?
- What form of business will be the easiest and least expensive to set up and maintain?

Choosing the legal form of your business is one of the most complex and critical decisions you'll need to make when organizing your new business. In the paragraphs that follow, we've outlined the various forms of organizing a business, but before making a decision you should discuss this issue thoroughly with an attorney or a tax accountant.

Sole Proprietorship

Sole proprietorship gives you complete control. You can establish this setup on the state level by registering your business under the Fictitious Names Act. On the federal level, you need only keep accurate accounting records and file a Schedule C (Profit or Loss from a Business or Profession) with your income taxes.

Under a sole proprietorship, you can't limit your personal liability against debt payment. Legal liability for defective products, professional malpractice, or any other claims also constitutes a personal liability. However, you can guard your business against these liabilities by insurance, as with any business. From a tax standpoint, it's usually advantageous to operate as a sole proprietor rather than to incorporate.

Partnership

Partnerships have many of the same advantages and disadvantages as sole proprietorships, except that there's more than one owner. A partnership requires minimal paperwork for state and federal authorities in order to be established. However, it's always a good idea for partners to have some form of written agreement about how they will share in the partnership's obligations, profits or losses, and capital. Without a partnership agreement, state laws will generally dictate the allocation of such items.

Some partnerships—especially limited partnerships set up for investment purposes—have a defined lifetime. How a partner joins or leaves the partnership, rights of interest purchased by other partners, terms of payment, and other such issues should be considered when drawing up partnership agreements.

Limited Partnership

When partners need more money than they can put into a venture themselves and either can't or don't want to borrow, they turn to a method of organization known as a limited partnership. Investors—known as limited partners—have the opportunity to own an equity position in the business. They have no say about how the business is run and are financially liable only up to the amount of their investment. The general partners manage the business and have full exposure to liability.

Corporation

Incorporating your business can be a costly and time-consuming process. State incorporation fees can cost hundreds or thousands of dollars.

There are also the ongoing expenses of maintaining and operating a corporation. Businesses are incorporated most often for the benefits of limited liability. In a corporation, the owners, officers, and directors are not usually personally liable for the company's debts.

S Corporation

S corporations can offer entrepreneurs the best of both worlds in many ways. S corporations aren't different from corporations under federal law and under some states' corporate laws. They offer owners the benefits of limited liability. In addition, there are usually no federal income taxes at the corporate level for S corporations. Profits or losses from S corporations flow directly through the company to the shareholders, thereby avoiding double taxation.

Limited Liability Company (LLC)

This business arrangement is accepted in most states and offers two major advantages: In contrast to partnerships, all members enjoy limited liability for the debts of the organization. Unlike corporations, an LLC does not incur the double income tax at the corporate and shareholder levels.

Financing Your Small Business

Some people have the capital to invest in a business without mortgaging their homes or other possessions. But most people who go into business for themselves need to raise at least some, if not most, of their start-up capital. In general, there are two types of funding sources: lenders and investors.

Lenders are generally commercial banks, corporate finance companies, and investment bankers. When lenders consider a loan request, they concentrate on what are sometimes referred to as the four Cs of credit: character, cash flow, collateral, and contribution (equity). Basically, lenders are looking for the company's ability to repay its debt. Investors, on the other hand, get a piece of the action (an equity position) in exchange for their monetary investment. In general, investors are less numbers driven than lenders because their reward structure is different.

You can also contact the Small Business Administration (SBA), a federal government agency that helps small businesses get started. Although people often talk about SBA loans, the agency doesn't lend its own money directly to consumers. Rather, you apply for an SBA loan through your commercial lender. The SBA then vouches for your creditworthiness by guaranteeing your loan at the bank.

Many entrepreneurs bypass the business loan altogether, however. Lenders often will not do business with you until you have a proven track record as a successful entrepreneur, so it's a catch-22 situation: Banks won't lend you the money to start your business because you don't have an established track record, but you can't develop a track record unless you have the needed capital to start the business.

If that's the situation you find yourself in, you might consider some nontraditional financing. One source: your family and friends. (See Chapter 1 for more details about borrowing from this source.) Other entrepreneurs tap their own resources by taking second mortgages on their homes, borrowing against their life insurance policies, or dipping into their retirement savings plans. (See Chapter 1 for more details about borrowing from your 401(k) plan.)

Your E&Y Planner Says:

No matter where you get the money, you stand to lose a great deal if the business doesn't thrive. But, as frightening as that proposition is, it's impractical to go into business for yourself without sufficient capital. I've seen some entrepreneurs go into business and then 18 months down the road realize they don't have enough capital. Their payments exceed their income and they're forced to shut down their operations. Other entrepreneurs try to minimize their financial risk by investing less start-up capital. That's a mistake. Not having the proper funding may prevent even the best idea from getting off the ground.

For a woman starting a new business, there are some particular concerns as well as opportunities. Ask yourself:

- Are you prepared to delay marriage or having a family?
- Have you considered the impact on your relationship with your spouse or life partner? Is your husband or life partner supportive of your new venture?
- What are the added costs, both emotional and financial, regarding your children? Will you need child care or other domestic help to cover for the time you will not be at home?

Numerous support and business groups exist for women entrepreneurs, however, and these can offer practical solutions for setting up a business and getting the necessary financing. For instance, Catalyst, a nonprofit group in New York City, offers information to entrepreneurial women on a variety of topics. The National Association of Women Business Owners in Silver Spring, Maryland, represents the interests of all women entrepreneurs in all types of businesses. The National Women's Business Center in Washington, DC, helps women entrepreneurs at all stages of business development. And the Small Business Administration's Office of Women's Business Ownership helps women start and build successful businesses. (See our Resources chapter for more information about these support groups.)

LOOKING AHEAD:
What You Should Be Doing Right Now

Whether you're starting a new business, acquiring an existing business, or buying a franchise, consider the following:

1. *Assess your personality.* Are you prepared to work hard and make less during the start-up phase of your business?
2. *Consider your options.* Whether you want to start your own business from scratch or acquire an existing business, each option has numerous advantages and drawbacks. Note which pros and cons seem most compelling, given your own personal situation.
3. *Develop a business plan.* This document takes time and energy to compile, but it's necessary to provide direction to your firm and to help raise needed capital.

4. *Choose the proper business structure.* Whether you choose a sole proprietorship or a corporation will determine whether you're personally liable for debts or claims made against the business.
5. *Consult with an attorney and a qualified accountant.* Running a business will leave you little time for keeping up with tax and legal changes that will affect your business.

LIFE AFTER WORK

W omen should be worried about a secure retirement—and with good reason. Consider the following:

- Women take time off to raise families and care for elderly parents. Married women who are currently retired or nearing retirement are less likely to have worked throughout their adult lives than their husbands. Married women are more likely to have worked part time or seasonally. This is also true for single, divorced, and widowed women with children.
- Women earn less money than men and work fewer years on average.
- Women change jobs more often than men. As a result, they frequently don't qualify for pensions or retirement plans. Women who are currently retired or nearing retirement are less likely to have been eligible for defined-benefit pensions than are men in their age groups.
- Women outlive men by 7 years on average.

All of these factors can lead to a very lean retirement. Is it any wonder women are more concerned than men about outliving their money?

To better prepare for retirement, women must understand what they have and how to make it last. If both you and your husband work, each of you must take responsibility for your own retirement planning and investing. If your husband works and you don't, you must understand what options your husband has for collecting his retirement benefits and how those options will affect you. (This is especially important if your husband dies or you get divorced.)

Unfortunately, the cross-your-fingers-and-wait-and-see approach isn't going to work. You need a plan—complete with goals, an expected retirement date, and a reasonable life expectancy. If you can't crunch these numbers yourself, visit a Web site such as MoneyAdvisor (www .moneyadvisor.com) or FinanCenter (www.financenter.com) that offers a retirement calculator. Ultimately, you may want a qualified financial planner to help you design a retirement plan. In the meantime, you can take the following steps to better prepare yourself for retirement:

Educate Yourself

A study done in 1998 showed that women midlife and older lacked adequate investing and retirement information. Forty-seven percent had little or no knowledge about mutual funds; 53% had little or no knowledge about stocks. Many of the women surveyed said they didn't seek advice from the investment community because they feared scams. Thus, 61% turn to newspapers and magazines and 59% look to friends and relatives.*

What's a woman to do, then? Going it alone or asking friends for investment advice is not the best plan of action. Rather, start learning (and doing) by using carefully planned books like this one, retirement planning software, and other educational materials from financial organizations and companies. You can also attend a financial planning seminar. (Many are designed specifically for women.) If there is any financial education offered through your place of employment, be sure to participate.

Pay Yourself First

This age-old advice still rings true today. Make paying yourself an expense, like the groceries and the telephone bill. Putting money away for a comfortable retirement is certainly as important an expense as these more immediate ones.

Still think you can't afford to save? The truth is, you can't afford *not* to save. Although Social Security will probably still be around when you retire, more than likely it will not provide the same level of benefits that

---

*Maturing Marketplace, June 1, 1998: "Women Lack Financial Planning Information; Marketers Must Wake Up, Study Says," Business Publishers, Inc.

it does today. In addition, even if you're eligible for benefits from a pension plan (either from your employer or through your spouse), pension benefits and Social Security will not be enough to meet your expenses in retirement. If you're not fortunate enough to be heir to a hefty inheritance, like most people, you must have a nest egg.

Let's assume that you've just decided you're going to save 6% of your $600 monthly salary to take advantage of your company's matching program, which matches dollar-for-dollar on the first 6%. Your contribution comes out to $9 per week: $9 per week times 52 weeks equals $468.00. (That's just the raw numbers without the company match and without any investment growth added.) Add a company match, and that $468 matched with the company's 6% would grow to $936 by year end—without you having done anything but put the money into your retirement savings account. Add a 10% rate of return, and that money would grow to $983 after 1 year.

Can you think of a painless way to find $9, or whatever amount equals 6% of your salary, per week? We can. Here's a list we use frequently in our financial education program. Find the suggestions that make sense for you:

- Make a budget to see where your money is going.
- Take a brown bag lunch to work and drink the coffee from the urn instead of buying it by the container.
- Pay your bills on time, and invest the interest you used to be charged for late payments.
- If you want to read that best-seller, borrow it from your local library.
- Cut back on eating out and ordering in. (You'll be surprised at how much you can save by cooking your own meals. And it's generally healthier for you, too.)
- Shop at the local grocery store that has the most reasonable prices, or become a member of a grocery co-op or price club. The rule of thumb for grocery purchases is that unless there's something you really like about a particular product and you believe there's a compelling reason to buy it (you love the scent of a brand-name air freshener, for instance), always buy the cheaper product or the generic brand. You'll save a lot this way, especially if you make use of those coupons most of us just toss in the garbage.
- Buy clothes off season, and shop the sales.
- Don't give away Junior's clothes if you're expecting to have another child.
- Do your own home repairs.

- Think about how much money you spend at the dry cleaner, and look for clothes you can wash. (Even silk is washable these days.)
- Rent a video instead of going to the movies.
- Beware of impulse purchases.
- Set up a separate account for your vacation.
- Give your children an allowance, instead of doling out money whenever they ask for it.
- Figure out how you can make your daily commute less expensive. Try walking at least part of the way if you can. The exercise is an added benefit.
- Cut back on your phone calls, especially if you have a cellular phone.

When you prepare your budget, we're sure you'll find other spending habits that let potential investment money slip through your fingers. (For a sample budget worksheet, see Chapter 1.) Once you start cutting back, you'll gain a sense of satisfaction knowing you're in control of your pocketbook. The point is: Pick an amount you want to save—the 6% mentioned earlier, for example—and then figure out how to get there. We find that once our clients get started they rarely feel any pinch from the money being siphoned into savings. To make your nest egg grow faster, increase your savings amount when you get a raise.

Start Your Own Retirement Account

You should open your own individual retirement account (IRA) or participate in a retirement plan at work. If you are a married woman who does not work outside the home, you can put up to $2,000 per year into an IRA. If you're able to participate in a retirement plan at work, the best way to take part is to have a portion of your paycheck automatically deducted and placed in your employer-sponsored 401(k), 403(b), or 457 plan. The advantages of this method of saving are clear:

- Once you authorize the deduction, you don't have to think about it anymore.
- Professional money managers make day-to-day decisions about your retirement funds at a fraction of what it would cost to hire your own money manager.
- Many companies match a portion of your contribution, which is like paying yourself twice. If you can't afford to put a lot of money into

your plan, try to put in just enough to receive your employer's full match.

- You don't have to pay taxes on this money until you retire, so the money grows tax free.
- You'll receive convenient quarterly account statements. In most cases, you'll have access to your account (and to a service representative) through a toll-free number.

You might also want to consider the new Roth IRA. Contributions are nondeductible for current tax purposes, but withdrawals are tax free in most cases. Many IRAs permit small opening balances, so you shouldn't worry about not having enough to open an account. If you're married and you open an IRA, be sure to find out about IRA rollover rules for surviving spouse beneficiaries and the new IRA rules on non-working spousal contributions.

MYTH   I've Missed the Boat. If Only I'd Started Saving Sooner . . .

Stop beating yourself up if you haven't started to save. Just make a commitment to start today. If you're age 25, waiting 1 year to save $10 per week could cost you over $12,000 in retirement. If you're age 40, a 1-year delay in saving $50 per week could cost you over $18,000 in retirement.

Take Advantage of Tax-Deferred Investment Earnings

A key advantage of saving in 401(k), 403(b), or 457 plans is that you do not have to pay taxes on your investment earnings as long as you keep your money in the plan. Income taxes are delayed until you take your money out of the plan, so money you would otherwise pay in taxes continues to grow for you. (See Figures 10.1 and 10.2 for an illustration of this savings advantage.)

Investment earnings are compounded before taxes are withdrawn. That means that saving on a before-tax, tax-deferred basis results in higher amounts available at retirement. More money stays in the account to grow. Let's look at an example, assuming:

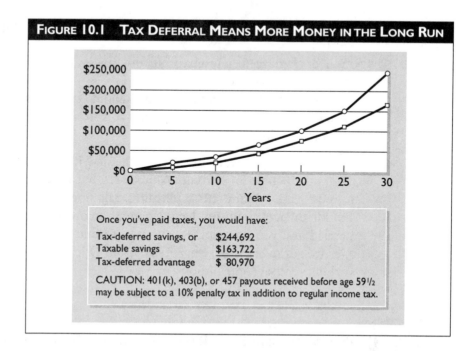

FIGURE 10.1   TAX DEFERRAL MEANS MORE MONEY IN THE LONG RUN

Once you've paid taxes, you would have:

Tax-deferred savings, or	$244,692
Taxable savings	$163,722
Tax-deferred advantage	$ 80,970

CAUTION: 401(k), 403(b), or 457 payouts received before age 59½ may be subject to a 10% penalty tax in addition to regular income tax.

FIGURE 10.2   401(K) PLANS VS. ORDINARY SAVINGS

Age of Investor	Amount of Monthly 401(k) Investment	Investor's Age at Time of Lump-Sum Withdrawal	Amount in 401(k) at Withdrawal	Rate at Which Amount Earned Is Taxed (Investor's Tax Bracket)	Amount of Lump-Sum Distribution after Taxes
40	$100	65	$81,212	15%	$69,000

VERSUS

Age of Investor	Amount of Monthly Contribution to a Savings Account	Taxed At	Rate of Interest	Investor's Age at Time of Lump-Sum Withdrawal	Amount Available for Retirement
40	$100	15%	7%	65	$58,876

$3,000 annual savings for 30 years

8% rate of return

28% tax rate

In this example, the tax-deferred savings advantage is $80,970.

Your E&Y Planner Says:

Although some women take advantage of saving through their 401(k) plans, the disturbing statistic is that women are much more likely than men to deplete lump-sum distributions from defined contribution plans. In 1992, only 34% of women nearing retirement (vs. 48% of men) retained their sums for retirement purposes by rolling them over to an IRA, leaving the money with their old employer, transferring the money to a new employer, or converting the lump-sum distribution to an annuity.* This kind of ill-advised spending contributes to women's financial hardships during retirement. They don't let their hard-earned dollars continue to grow for them. The reasons behind this behavior are probably complex, but the single answer may be that women are still uncomfortable with investing and so start living off the lump sum with no investment plan.

Consider Taking More Investment Risk

Although it is important to be comfortable with the level of investment risk you take, over the long term greater risk may help you earn more for retirement. According to the 1997 Dreyfus Gender Investment Comparison Study, female respondents said they are less likely to take risk in investments than men and tend to be more anxious about the investments they do own. Sixty-three percent of the women said they only consider safe and guaranteed investments, compared with 41% of men surveyed.

*Sophie Korczyk, Pre-Retirement Pension Distributions in the Health and Retirement Study, August 1996.

Know Your Retirement Rights

In most cases, a woman is guaranteed to continue to receive a portion of her husband's pension if he dies before her. Under the Employee Retirement and Income Security Act of 1974 (ERISA), a wife must sign a waiver to give up these rights. Sometimes a couple decides to do this because they will receive a higher monthly income stream while the husband is alive under a single-life annuity versus a joint and survivor annuity. Because statistically your husband will likely die before you, you must understand that if you waive your rights, his pension benefits will cease when he dies.

Assert Your Financial Independence

If you are a working woman, it is important that you manage your own retirement fund. Even if you allow your spouse or life partner to manage the other investment and financial planning for the household, you should control your retirement money. It's important that each of you diversify within your own retirement account, rather than diversifying as a household. Why? If you should divorce or separate from a life partner, and you've agreed to hold the conservative part of the retirement portfolio, you'll be left with a fund that is more than likely worth a lot less than the fund of your spouse or life partner.

In addition, you may want to consult separately with your own financial planner. Creating personal relationships with a group of professionals is important for you now and in the future. There is a growing list of women in the financial planning field who specialize in working with women on retirement planning, as well as in handling the financial transition necessary after the death of a spouse or a life partner. (See the Resources chapter at the back of the book.)

OTHER SOURCES OF RETIREMENT INCOME

Besides the income from your investments (which, by the way, is where the majority of your retirement income will come from), Social Security and pension plans will help to subsidize your retirement.

Your E&Y Planner Says:

Retirement planning is a hot topic these days. Everybody is talking about it. The White House just had a summit on it. (Ernst & Young was there, of course.) Bookstores and libraries offer dozens of volumes on the subject. (Ernst & Young is there, too.)

But so much talk can be confusing. How much money do women really need? And how should they accumulate those funds?

The degree of confusion hit home when I met with Annette, who was in her 50s and newly divorced. She had three grown kids and two teenagers, and she'd just read an article in a personal finance magazine that said she needed $5 million to retire comfortably.

Annette didn't have $5 million. She was frantic. How would she take care of herself and the children?

Annette's divorce agreement from her executive husband included her house, half her husband's pension, generous child support (including all college costs), and $1 million in cash. Annette was a naturally frugal person; she and her children were living on her $40,000 teacher's salary. She was banking the child support and had already put the $1 million into Treasuries.

Annette was in no danger of running out of money unless she suffered some catastrophic illness. Her teacher's union had long-term care and catastrophic policies at a reasonable cost, which would insure her against this risk. But the magazine had said $5 million, and she didn't have it. I ran the numbers for her, talked to her about long-term care and health insurance, and discussed diversifying a bit out of Treasuries. Annette didn't need to worry. But I understand why she did.

FACT

You Can Check Up on Your Social Security Benefits

To make sure your benefits and your spouse's benefits are accruing properly, you can request a copy of your Earnings and Benefit Estimate Statement from the Social Security Administration. It's free when you call their toll-free number (800-772-1213). You can fix any mistakes and make sure they have up-to-date information about your earnings history.

Many of our clients don't know that the rules about normal retirement age have already changed, however (see Figure 10.3). If you decide to start collecting Social Security benefits before your normal retirement age, you'll get a reduced benefit. You can start taking reduced benefits at age 62.

If you've been working full time, find out what kind of pension income you can expect from your employer. Most companies will do a projection for you. If not, you can get the formula they use to do their calculations and either run the numbers yourself or ask your financial

FIGURE 10.3 SOCIAL SECURITY NORMAL RETIREMENT AGE	
Year of Birth	**Normal Retirement Age**
Before 1938	65
1938	65 and 2 months
1939	65 and 4 months
1940	65 and 6 months
1941	65 and 8 months
1942	65 and 10 months
1943–1954	66
1955	66 and 2 months
1956	66 and 4 months
1957	66 and 6 months
1958	66 and 8 months
1959	66 and 10 months
1960 and later	67

Source: Social Security Administration (www.ssa.gov)

planner to help you. Don't forget to check with prior employers to see if you'll receive a pension from them as well. Some employers send out periodic personalized benefit statements that include pension projection information. Factor this amount in with the income you will receive from Social Security and your investments.

> ## MYTH Social Security Calculates Your Benefit Using Your Last 5 to 10 Years' Wage History
>
> Social Security provides a retirement benefit to nonworking as well as working spouses. To qualify for a Social Security benefit on your own wage history, you need to have worked at least 40 quarters. (They don't have to be consecutive, however.) If you have your own wages, your Social Security benefit will be based on whichever calculation produces a higher benefit: your wage history or a percentage of your spouse's earnings. Social Security uses up to 35 years of your highest wage history to calculate your benefit. Often, taxpayers assume that the government calculates your benefit using just the last 5 or 10 years of work, so if you haven't worked lately or if you work part time, you won't get Social Security. That's simply not true. Your Social Security benefit is an average of your working life, up to 35 years.

OTHER ISSUES

Some other issues that may concern you during your retirement include deciding where to retire and starting a second career.

Where Will You Live?

Many retirees relocate from their homes to other areas of the country that are less expensive. Others relocate based on other factors, such as a more agreeable climate or to be near loved ones. Many simply stay put, of course, either because they like where they live or because friends and family live nearby.

Once you have estimated what your postretirement income will be, you'll know where you can afford to live. That may mean you'll have to save more, or perhaps invest a bit more aggressively, in order to be able to live where you wish (see Figure 10.4).

(Keep in mind that if you move to another state, the laws regarding the division of marital property and the validity of prenuptial agreements may differ from the state in which you currently live. Ask your attorney if you're concerned about these issues.)

A CASE STUDY: MAKING THE BIG MOVE

Leo was scheduled to retire from his factory job in 2 years. His wife, Mary, a homemaker, was worried they wouldn't be able to afford their current lifestyle. Given their retirement savings and current living expenses, Mary was right to be concerned. So I suggested that they consider moving from their suburban New York home to a more affordable area of the country.

Mary and Leo contacted a national realty chain to help them find a community that matched their income and their personal needs. After doing some research, they decided to investigate Arkansas.

Mary and Leo used their vacation to check out several of Arkansas' prime retirement areas—Hot Springs Village, Benton County, Fayetteville, Harrison, and Mountain Home-Bull Shoals. They questioned local real estate agents and residents about the weather, entertainment options, recreational areas, houses of worship, medical care, housing costs, and taxes to get a feel for the various communities. Both were pleasantly surprised to learn that Arkansas residents were among the least taxed in the country, ranking 49th per capita in state and local taxes, with the average resident paying $1,334 a year compared to $2,038 for the nation. They also learned that some of the communities they visited were among the top 10 retirement areas for low property taxes. Mountain Home-Bull Shoals, where Mary and Leo decided to settle, was listed in one study as one of the safest retirement communities in the country.

Does this mean that Arkansas is the ideal retirement place for everyone? Of course not. The point is, you need to plan where you'll spend your retirement years, even if that plan means you'll stay right where you are. Another client, Anne, who has chosen the single lifestyle, owns a co-op apartment in a large city. Her passion is art, so she's always loved the city because she likes to visit the galleries and museums. While the

---

FIGURE 10.4   RELOCATION CHECKLIST

Financial Issues to Consider

State taxes
Real estate prices
Local taxes
Real estate property taxes
Sales tax
Auto insurance rates
Medical care and prescription drug costs
Vehicle registration fee
Driver's license fee
Health insurance
Food costs
Clothing costs
Entertainment costs
Travel costs to visit your children

Nonfinancial Issues to Consider

Crime rate
Recreation facilities
Senior activities
Religious organizations
Pace of life
Climate
Volunteer organizations
Proximity to a college, city, or hospital
Access to public transportation
Proximity to ambulance care
Part-time work availability
Proximity to family and friends
Overall environment (urban, suburban, rural, etc.)

---

cost of living in a large city can be high—especially on a retiree's budget—Anne was determined to make it work. She felt that giving up her city lifestyle would make her retirement years miserable. Because she had lived in the same apartment for 30 years and now owns it, she can make her retirement dream come true.

Starting a Second Career

If you find you're coming up short financially, a second career may be one way to supplement your retirement income. Depending upon the type of work you decide to pursue, a second career can be personally satisfying as well as financially rewarding.

Statistics show, in fact, that the productivity level of older workers in most jobs is just as high as that of other age groups. Employers appreciate the experience level of older workers and like the fact that the attendance records of older workers are equal to or better than those of most other age groups.

Before you make the leap back into the workforce, take some time to think about what working after retirement really means. Are you ready to take orders from a boss again? Will you work full time or part time? How will earning a salary affect your Social Security benefits? If you have a spouse or life partner, discuss how continuing to work will affect his or her retirement plans. A few of the pros and cons you might want to consider are listed in Figure 10.5.

HEALTH CARE AND LIFE INSURANCE NEEDS

Health Care

Your health care costs will probably change after you retire. Your medical needs and out-of-pocket expenses, for example, will go up as your health changes. In addition, your share of premium contributions for medical benefits from your employer and Medicare can be expected to go up. Coverage from these sources could change in other ways, too, and you may end up paying substantially more out of your own pocket.

Many women erroneously believe that they don't need to worry about health insurance once they retire because they will have Medicare. Although Medicare does cover many of your health insurance needs after you turn 65, coverage is limited. You must pay deductibles and copayments—and not all doctors accept Medicare as payment in full. Custodial care, the type of care most commonly required by those in a nursing home, is not covered by Medicare. Nor are prescription drugs.

To cover these limitations, you may need to purchase Medigap insurance. Medigap policies, which are sold by private insurance companies, are designed to fill the gaps between Medicare benefits and the coverage

---

FIGURE 10.5 IS A SECOND CAREER RIGHT FOR YOU?

Advantages of a Second Career

Personal satisfaction
Opportunity to learn something new and mingle with a variety of
people
Self-esteem booster
Additional income

Disadvantages of a Second Career

Conflicts with retirement plans of spouse or life partner
Additional costs, such as work clothing, lunch, and commuting
Job-related stress
Loss of leisure time
Possible reduction of Social Security benefits

---

you desire. Federal law requires that insurers offer no more than 10 standard Medigap policies. Each policy must provide at least a core of basic benefits. A plan with only the core benefits is designated Plan A, and each policy in the succession of standard plans—designated B through J—adds more benefits to the core. When shopping for a Medigap policy, select the policy that includes the benefits you think you'll need.

Here's a suggested assumption you might want to make in your retirement planning: If you retire before age 65, project that your annual medical expenses during retirement will cost you around $6,000 per year, and that these expenses will grow at a faster rate than your other expenses. These costs will probably decrease by approximately half when you reach age 65 because you become eligible for Medicare. If you're married, you should project the same level of expenses for your spouse.

Medicare Provides Comprehensive Health Insurance

The truth is, Medicare does *not* cover:

- Care in a skilled nursing facility beyond 100 days per benefit period
- Custodial care (the type of care most commonly required by those in nursing homes)

- Out-of-pocket costs for prescription drugs
- Medical tests for (and the cost of) eyeglasses or hearing aids
- Care received outside of the United States

Life Insurance

You will continue to need some life insurance after you retire. Some women find that they don't need quite as much insurance as they did during their prime working years. The mortgage may be paid off, and the children are probably living on their own (and no longer depending upon parents for support). In this situation, you may want to reduce your coverage. The benefit, of course, is that you'll save on premiums. You can use this extra cash to cover medical expenses or a long-term care insurance policy. (See Chapter 5 for more information on long-term care policies.)

Other women, however, discover that their insurance needs aren't diminished all that much in retirement. A sizable insurance policy may still be needed to provide adequate income for the surviving spouse. Consider what the surviving spouse's cash flow and capital would look like if you or your spouse were to die tomorrow. Would you be able to live in comfort financially if your spouse were to die?

Your need for a substantial life insurance policy (for you and your husband) will continue in retirement if your retirement income will be derived from a pension and Social Security. Upon your husband's death, the pension benefit payable to you might decrease by as much as 50% depending on the plan. (The same is true for your husband on your death.) The Social Security benefit paid to you as a surviving spouse will likely decrease too.

Review your life insurance needs periodically. If your spouse or life partner dies, consider cutting back your coverage to a small policy that will cover your funeral expenses and the cost of settling your estate. (See Chapter 5 for life insurance needs before retirement.)

RETIRING WITH YOUR LIFE PARTNER

If you have a life partner (as opposed to a spouse), you must take certain precautions to ensure that you have a comfortable retirement, particularly if your life partner were to die or end the relationship. Although it is likely that your life partner will name you as the beneficiary of his or her life insurance policies and 401(k), 403(b), or 457 savings plans, and it's possible, but unlikely, for you to be named as the beneficiary of your partner's pension, it's not possible for you to be named as the beneficiary of your partner's Social Security benefits. That means that if your partner dies, and his or her pension and Social Security were a sizable portion of your collective retirement benefits, you may be left with a substantial dent in your postretirement income. There are several strategies you can employ (which we discuss in Chapter 4) to protect yourself in this situation. One of the smartest strategies, however, is to save for your own retirement as if you were a single woman.

LOOKING AHEAD:
What You Should Be Doing Right Now

You probably have some planning to do. But if you take things one step at a time, you'll find that you have a lot more control over your future. (And you can stop crossing your fingers.)

1. *Take the first steps in preparing for your retirement by educating yourself* about the general issue of retirement, opening up your own retirement account, and understanding your retirement rights.
2. *Complete a financial planning worksheet.* It'll give you a quick snapshot of your current retirement plan.
3. *Consult a qualified financial planner* to help you design a retirement plan that works for you.
4. *List your income sources after retirement.* Include how much you expect from each source and when you expect to receive those funds. This will help you determine where the gaps are. Calculate these figures for yourself and your husband or life partner separately.
5. *If you'll be retiring with your spouse,* but you haven't worked much outside the home, be sure you understand the income options for you alone as well as for you and your husband as a couple.
6. *Familiarize yourself with your spouse's or life partner's benefits.* Obtain summary plan descriptions from the human resources department.

Make sure you read all benefit communications mailed to your home.

7. *Join your spouse or life partner in any retirement counseling sessions* offered by his or her employer.

8. *Review all of the primary, secondary, and contingency beneficiary designations currently in effect* in all plans to determine if they are consistent with your overall estate planning. Consult an estate planning attorney for guidance with these plans.

9. *Check with all prior employers* to see if either you or your spouse has any vested pension benefits due and/or survivor benefits available at the time of death. Find out the exact procedure necessary to claim such benefits.

10. *If you plan to retire before age 65,* and both you and your spouse are covered under his employer-sponsored health care plan, retain coverage under COBRA when your spouse retires, even if he will be covered by Medicare.

11. *Switch household financial responsibilities* (such as balancing the checkbook, paying bills, and monitoring investments) for at least 1 month, so that both you and your husband or life partner are familiar with and appreciate the tasks each of you performs regarding finances.

12. *If you work, manage your own retirement fund.* If you have not worked outside the home, start and manage your own IRA. Don't leave all of the money management to your spouse or life partner.

13. *Diversify within your own retirement portfolio,* not just as a household.

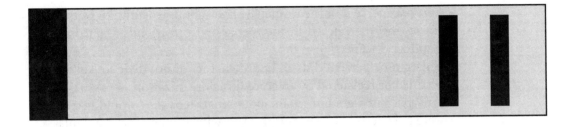

NEXT STEPS

FACT   **The financial services industry has spent millions of dollars in an effort to reach women investors.**

MYTH   **Women have all the information they need about money management, investing, and retirement.**

According to a recent study of 500 midlife and older women by the National Center for Women and Aging at Brandeis University, women lack the basic information needed to manage their finances. Although these women realize that financial professionals could offer the necessary guidance and support to educate them about such matters, they still are often reluctant to seek professional help. Of the women surveyed, a large percentage of those who had worked with a financial consultant did not have information about their planner's credentials, the service fee structure, or where to turn if faced with a serious problem. The survey also discovered that:

- Fifty percent of the women who had not consulted a financial professional said they did not know how to select someone who would be likely to give them good, competent advice.

- Forty-six percent of the women worried about trusting advisors due to stories they had heard in the media or from friends about financial frauds and scams.
- Thirty-nine percent did not know whether or not their consultant was certified or registered by an accrediting organization.
- Fifty percent were uncertain about what steps they would take if they were to experience a serious problem with a financial consultant.

Since the very first page of this book, we've been telling you—whether you're married, single, divorced, or widowed—that you must take control of your financial future. That doesn't necessarily mean, however, that you must do so alone. In many cases, it may be a smart idea to hire a reliable adviser who can help you devise your game plan. That's especially true if you are confronted with a new life stage such as widowhood, divorce, or marriage.

A good financial adviser—whether a financial planner, an insurance agent, a tax accountant, or a stockbroker—can offer information and advice on how to spend and save your money. Even if you understand the basics of financial planning, you may still need an adviser to help you make sense of the broad array of choices available today. For example, what type of life insurance policy fits your needs? When it comes to investing, there are literally thousands of different mutual funds available that invest in everything from small company stocks to foreign currencies. Dozens of different kinds of bonds exist. And an even greater number of companies and government entities sell shares of their stock or debt on the public exchanges. A reliable financial adviser can help define your goals and your needs and help you make a plan and meet it.

But who should you hire for this task? How do you know that he or she is the best person for the job? And what exactly can you expect him or her to do for you? Here are some guidelines that can help you answer these questions.

Selecting a Financial Planner

A financial planner helps you understand your financial situation, set your financial goals, and develop and implement strategies to help you meet those goals. He or she can advise you on a complex financial matter such as setting up a trust, or simply help you set up a workable budget and savings plan. He or she can focus solely on a single issue, such as retirement planning, or help you devise a comprehensive plan that covers every aspect of your financial future. A financial planner can also help you implement your strategies by working with and coordinating the efforts of your attorney, insurance agent, and investment adviser to make sure all the details are taken care of.

At your first meeting or two, a good financial planner will assess your current financial situation. What assets do you have, for instance? How much have you already saved for retirement? Next, he or she will ask about short- and long-term goals. When do you hope to retire? Do you expect to pay for your children's college tuition? Finally, he or she will question you to help you determine your risk tolerance. If you invest a portion of your funds in the stock market, for instance, how upset will you be if the market dips a few points? Based upon this information, your planner will develop an appropriate strategy to meet your goals.

If you want the planner to draw up a comprehensive financial plan for you (rather than simply finding solutions to a particular problem), you can expect the plan to cover everything from a budget to investments to estate planning. Recommendations should be made for certain types of investments (along with their future projected returns). As well, your planner should make sure your portfolio is diversified and that you have sufficient insurance coverage. If you want the relationship to be ongoing, the planner will monitor your financial situation periodically. You'll probably meet at least once a year to review your goals and to make any necessary adjustments to your strategy.

To find a good financial planner you can trust, ask your lawyer, friends, family, and co-workers for referrals. Talk to people who have similar backgrounds or needs: If you want to retire early and plan for your child's college education, for example, you don't want a planner who works primarily with small business owners. There are many types of financial planners, often making it difficult to choose the appropriate person. One way to distinguish among the crowd is to find out how the planner is paid. A *fee-only* planner, for instance, is paid solely for his or her advice. He or she does not receive a commission for any recommended investments that you purchase. The fee can be a percentage of your portfolio, a per-hour charge, or a flat fee for the entire plan. For a list of fee-only planners in your area, contact the National Association of Personal Financial Advisors (888-FEE-ONLY, www.napfa.org). A *commission-based* planner provides financial advice, too. But he or she can also sell you the products you need to meet your goals, such as an insurance policy or a mutual fund. The chief advantage of this arrangement is that it provides one-stop shopping. The disadvantage is that basing a planner's fee on commissions may raise questions about his or her objectivity. Is the mutual fund the planner recommended a good investment for you—or is there another fund that is a better fit that he or she doesn't know about (or won't recommend) because he or she can't sell it? The *fee-based* planner, a hybrid of the fee-only and commission-only planner, charges a fee for advice and in addition may receive a commission for any investments he or she recommends. A *fee-offset* planner will charge you for advice initially. But that fee may be offset against commissions the planner receives later on when you buy recommended investments.

Your E&Y Planner Says:

If you're just starting out and your assets are small, a fee-based planner may be disproportionately expensive. At this stage in your life, you may want to work with a commission-based or fee-offset planner.

Interview at least three of the planners you've been referred to. Ask them about their compensation as well as their experience and credentials. Look for advisers or planners who have one or more of the following designations, especially if they have their own firms or work at small companies. None of these designations are exactly seals of approval, but the fact that a planner has undergone a lengthy (and often difficult) course of study is significant.

Personal Financial Specialist

A personal financial specialist is a certified public accountant who is trained in personal finance. This designation, given by the American Institute of Certified Public Accountants (AICPA), is granted to CPAs who have passed a 6-hour test and have had at least 3 years of experience in financial planning. Consumers can contact AICPA (888-999-9256, www.aicpa.org) for a list of CPAs who have earned the PFS designation.

Certified Financial Planner (CFP)

A certified financial planner must complete a rigorous certification exam. Afterward, he or she must complete 30 hours of continuing education every 2 years. The trademark license is awarded by the Certified Financial Planner Board of Standards. Consumers can contact the Board (888-CFP-MARK, www.cfp-board.org) to confirm whether a financial planner is currently licensed, to determine whether a CFP licensee has ever been disciplined by the CFP board, to lodge a complaint against a CFP practitioner, or to receive general information and brochures about financial planning.

For a list of 3 CFPs in your area, contact the Institute of Certified Financial Planners (800-282-7526, www.icfp.org), a professional membership organization of more than 12,500 people who either are CFPs or are working toward receiving that designation. You can also contact the International Association for Financial Planning (888-806-PLAN, www.iafp.org) for free brochures about financial planning and detailed disclosure forms on up to 5 local financial advisors.

Chartered Financial Consultant (ChFC)

A chartered financial consultant has completed the American College's 10-course financial planning ChFC education program. ChFCs must have at least 3 years of practical industry experience. The American Society of CLU & ChFC (800-392-6900, www.agents-online.com/ASCLU/index .html) will provide names of planners in your area.

You can check up on a financial planner's history, qualifications, and possible conflicts of interest using a document called Form ADV. Planners who provide investment advice are required to file this form with federal regulators and their state securities department. Part I of this form discloses any legal or financial difficulties the planner has had as well as any disciplinary action that regulators may have taken against him or her.

Hiring a Stockbroker

If you plan to invest in a no-load mutual fund, you can generally do that on your own or with the help of a fee-only financial planner. But if you want to invest in individual stocks, bonds, and other securities on the open market, in most cases you need a stockbroker to handle the transaction for you.

A stockbroker earns his or her income through the commissions paid on the investments you buy or sell. The more stocks you buy and sell—the more frequently you do so—the more your broker will earn in commissions.

A *full-service* stockbroker typically earns the highest commissions because he or she offers investment advice, too. This type of broker will tell you which stocks to pick and advise you about long-term investment strategies and risks. He or she will provide periodic updates on your portfolio's performance and send you reports from the brokerage's research analysts.

If you want to lower your commissions, consider using a *discount* brokerage house. These brokers don't offer advice about what to buy or sell, but they can generally still send you some research information, and many of the larger discounters offer walk-in offices. You'll lower your fees by up to 70%.

Deep-discount brokers offer even fewer services. Most deep discounters do not have walk-in offices and deal with customers by phone only. The price is low, sometimes 90% less than what a full-service broker would charge. For a similarly low price, you could execute your own trades directly over the Internet with one of the growing number of on-line brokerages.

As with financial planners, ask for referrals from friends and relatives. Check with the National Association of Securities Dealers Regulation (800-289-9999, www.nasdr.com) to make sure that the broker is licensed to operate in your state and that he or she has not had any complaints or disciplinary action filed against him or her. To find out if a broker has committed fraud or any other serious violations, review his or her Central Registration Depository (CRUD) file. Most states will provide some of this information over the phone and then follow it up with a copy of the actual CRUD report. Other states require a written request.

FINDING AN INSURANCE AGENT

According to the National Insurance Institute, some 2,600 insurance companies currently sell homeowners' and auto insurance in the United States. Another 1,700 or so companies sell life insurance. All insurance companies rely heavily on agents, who work on a commission basis, to sell their products.

Exclusive agents represent just one insurance company, whereas *independent agents* represent several companies. Exclusive agents may be able to get you a better price because they earn less in commission than independent agents. But independent agents can quote you the rates and terms on a variety of policies offered by different insurers.

To find an agent, contact the American Society of CLU & ChFC at 888-CHFC-CLU. They'll refer up to five chartered life insurance underwriters in your area. Most states require that agents be licensed to sell insurance. (Contact your state department of insurance.) Agents who sell variable life insurance (these policies invest some of your premiums into stocks, bonds, etc.) must also be registered with the National Association of Securities Dealers Regulation (800-289-9999).

You can also buy insurance directly from some insurance companies. In some states, savings banks can sell life insurance to consumers. Most employers, credit unions, and professional associations offer group coverage (to individuals) that is far less expensive than any policy you could buy on your own. (Contact the Credit Union National Association at 800-358-5710 for details about credit unions you can join.) And, if you want to comparison shop by phone, call one of the following computerized price quote services. You provide some personal information, and the service will provide four or five of the least expensive policies (monitored by its staff) that meet your needs. This service is usually free of charge. You can buy a policy from these companies, but you're not obligated to do so.

- Insurance Quote Services: 800-972-1104, www.iquote.com
- SelectQuote Insurance Services: 800-343-1985, www.selectquote.com
- TermQuote: 800-444-8376, www.term-quote.com

SELECTING AN ATTORNEY

An attorney is a licensed professional who can advise and represent you in legal matters. Although many attorneys still operate as general practitioners who can handle just about any type of legal case, most attorneys these days specialize in one or two areas such as domestic relations, taxation, or real estate. If you want to set up a trust, for instance, you'll need an attorney who specializes in estate planning. An attorney can help in the following areas:

Marriage and Divorce

An attorney can draw up separation agreements and negotiate divorce settlements. He or she can advise you about prenuptial agreements and custody arrangements, and can even negotiate adoption proceedings.

Estate Planning

An attorney can execute your will and counsel you on estate planning. He or she can set up trusts that will protect your assets and/or reduce your estate taxes.

Purchasing a Home

An attorney can represent you when you buy or sell a home. If you are selling a home, your attorney will prepare the contract of sale. If you're buying a home, he or she will review the contract of sale and negotiate the terms with the seller's attorney.

Taxes

An attorney can advise you about your tax obligations—everything from your federal income taxes to real estate taxes to inheritance and estate taxes. He or she can also advise you on the consequences of capital gains on real estate; sales of appreciated stock; bequests to your husband and children; and pensions, annuities, and trusts.

Personal Finances

An attorney can help you restructure your debt by arranging for a debt consolidation loan or contacting your creditors and getting an extension on your loan payments. He or she can also help you clean up your credit file, and, if necessary, counsel you on a bankruptcy filing.

As with planners and other financial advisors, you should ask friends, relatives, and co-workers for referrals. You can also call your local or state bar association for referrals. The association usually runs an attorney referral and information service.

Typically, attorneys bill individuals by the hour. Some charge a fixed fee for a routine job such as drafting a will. Many ask for some money up front (this is called a *retainer*). Contingency fees are paid to an attorney contingent upon the outcome of a case. That means the attorney has agreed to accept as his or her fee a percentage of the money the client wins in the case settlement. This type of fee is generally used in negligence cases involving personal injury.

All attorneys must have a bachelor's degree from an accredited college and a law degree from an accredited law school. An attorney is licensed by the state in which he or she wants to work. That doesn't mean he or she can practice law in every state, however: He or she must petition for admission to practice in another state.

A number of states and private organizations now certify attorneys who specialize in certain areas of practice. While requirements vary, most programs include the following components: substantial involvement, continuing legal education, peer review, and a written examination. The American Bar Association (ABA) has accredited 10 lawyer certification programs sponsored by private organizations, including the American Board of Certification's programs in business and consumer bankruptcy, and creditor's right, the National Board of Trial Advocacy's programs in civil and criminal trial advocacy, and other programs in estate planning law, elder law, and professional liability. Further information on both state and private certification programs for lawyers is available from the ABA's Standing Committee on Specialization (www.abanet.org/specialization).

WHEN YOU NEED A TAX ACCOUNTANT

You can prepare your own tax return. But if your return is complicated by a lot of deductions or special situations, you may want to hire a professional to help you. You have several options.

A Certified Public Accountant (CPA)

A CPA is licensed by the state. To earn his or her title, a CPA must work under an established CPA's supervision for 2 years and pass a rigorous exam that takes 2½ days to complete. Many CPAs can prepare your tax returns, recommend tax planning strategies, provide personal financial planning advice, and offer much of the same assistance an attorney provides. A CPA can be especially helpful if you are being audited by the Internal Revenue Service or if you need in-depth advice about the tax implications of starting and running a business. Be sure to ask about the CPA's experience, however. A CPA who specializes in these areas is probably a great choice, but a CPA who specializes in performing audits for companies would not be. To find a CPA in your area, call your state CPA society.

A National Tax Preparation Chain

National chains like H&R Block have offices set up all over the world. Most customers are helped on a first-come, first-serve basis. Fees are low, mostly because these companies don't provide financial planning assistance throughout the year and don't typically deal with complex tax returns.

An Enrolled Agent

An enrolled agent doesn't sell life insurance. Nor does he or she work for the Internal Revenue Service. Rather, an enrolled agent is a tax specialist who has worked for the IRS in some tax-related job for at least 5 years or passed a rigorous 2-day exam given by the IRS. To find an enrolled agent in your area, contact the National Association of Enrolled Agents (800-424-4339).

Whoever you choose, you will save time and money if you work with the same tax preparer each year because he or she will know your situation and how any tax changes might affect you.

Questions for a Financial Adviser

The best way to find any type of financial adviser is through a personal reference. Ask other advisers, your friends, co-workers, and relatives for the names of advisers they have worked with in the past. It's important to make sure your situation, issues, and concerns are similar to those of the people you ask for referrals. Ask other professionals with whom you already have a working relationship for references, too. Your financial planner may be able to recommend a stockbroker, for instance; your banker may be able to recommend an attorney; and so forth.

In addition, you can get referrals from professional organizations, such as the National Association of Personal Financial Advisors and the Institute of Certified Public Accountants, that operate nationwide. Being a member in good standing doesn't guarantee that an adviser will do a good job, of course. Look for organizations that require members to take exams and/or continuing education classes rather than simply to sign up and pay annual dues.

After you've compiled a short list of names, arrange to meet each adviser in person. Initial consultations are typically offered gratis because it gives you and the adviser the opportunity to see if you're compatible. Did you feel comfortable talking to this financial planner, for instance? Did he or she use a lot of business jargon, or did he or she speak in terms you could easily understand? Did the planner seem eager to answer your questions, or did he or she do most of the talking? Did you trust him or her? Could you imagine discussing your financial affairs in detail with him or her?

Before retaining an adviser's services, ask the following questions:

1. What is your background? What professional designations do you have? Do you belong to any professional organizations?
2. How long have you worked in this profession? What areas do you specialize in?
3. How do you get paid (by the hour, by the project, etc.)? How much do you charge? How long do you expect this work to take?
4. How much, if anything, will you and your firm earn on my investments?

5. What kinds of problems do you handle most frequently? Have you ever handled a situation and/or problem like mine?
6. What can I expect from you in terms of service?
7. How often will we meet? How will we communicate?
8. What percentage of your clients are women?
9. Can I speak with a few of your clients who are or were in situations similar to mine?
10. Have you ever been suspended or reprimanded for your business practices?
11. What other professionals will I need to retain to implement your advice? Will you take responsibility for coordinating the activities of these professionals?

RESOURCES

While Ernst & Young does not endorse the following resources, we believe most will be helpful in providing information, ideas, and assistance.

Organizations

Catalyst (120 Wall Street, 5th Floor, New York, NY 10005, 212-514-7600) is a national research and advisory organization that works with corporations to promote the careers of women. It offers publications on a variety of topics.

The Mutual Fund Education Alliance (100 NW Englewood Road, Suite 130, Kansas City, MO 64118, 816-454-9422, www.mfea.com) is a not-for-profit trade association that provides educational information about mutual fund investing.

The National Funeral Directors Association can provide you with funeral and burial pricing information. They can be reached at 414-789-1880, www.nfda.org.

The Widowed Persons Service (601 E Street NW, Washington, DC 20048, 202-434-2260) offers support for widows and others in bereavement. It also offers legal and financial counseling services.

If you are heavily in debt, contact the National Foundation for Consumer Credit. Their 1,300 member offices, which often operate under the name "Consumer Credit Counseling Service," offer free or low-cost counseling. They'll create a workable budget and repayment plan for you. Contact Consumer Credit Counseling Service, 8611 Second Avenue, Suite 100, Silver Spring, MD 20910, 800-388-2227, www.nfcc.org.

Contact the National Insurance Consumer Helpline (800-942-4242) for information about how to buy life insurance and other types of insurance.

To find an estate planning attorney, contact The National Network of Estate Planning Attorneys, 410 17th Street, Suite 1260, Denver, CO 80202, 800-638-8681.

The National Women's Business Center (1250 24th Street, NW, Suite 350, Washington, DC 20037, 202-466-0544, www.womenconnect.com/womensbusinesscenter) offers programs for women entrepreneurs.

The Small Business Administration's Office of Women's Business Ownership (202-205-6673, http://www.sba.gov/womeninbusiness/) offers nearly 70 women's business centers in 40 states to help women start and build successful businesses.

The National Association for Women Business Owners (1100 Wayne Avenue, Suite 830, Silver Spring, MD 20910, 301-608-2590, http://www.nawbo.org/nawbo/nawbostart.nsf) is a national organization of women entrepreneurs with over 60 chapters.

Brochures

The American Association of Retired Persons (800-424-3410, www.aarp.org) offers two informative planning guides that may help you decide about a second career: "Returning to the Job Market: A Woman's Guide to Employment Planning," and "Working Options—How to Plan: Your Job Search, Your Work Life."

Contact your State Insurance Department for a copy of "Shopper's Guide to Long Term Care Insurance," produced by the National Association of Insurance Commissioners.

For more information about Social Security Benefits, contact the Social Security Administration (800-772-1213, www.ssa.gov). You can request these pamphlets: "Understanding Social Security" (SSA 05-10024), or "Disability" (SSA 05-10029), or "What Every Woman Should Know" (SSA 05-10127).

The IRS (800-829-3676) offers free publications: "Federal Estate and Gift Taxes" (Publication 448), "Survivors, Executors and Administrators" (Publication 559), and "Tax Information for Divorced or Separated Individuals" (Publication 504). The IRS also operates a staffed tax hotline at 800-829-1040.

"What You Should Know About Buying Life Insurance" is offered free by the American Council of Life Insurance (1001 Pennsylvania Avenue NW, 5th Floor, Washington, DC, 20004, 202-624-2000).

WEB SITES

The Women's Network (www.ivillage.com). Perhaps the most well known women's Internet site, iVillage has an online community of over 500,000. Popular features include message boards, chat sessions, and classifieds.

MoneyMode on Women's Wire (www.womenswire.com/money). Co-sponsored by Bloomberg. Covers everything from how to invest your money to debt, taxes, and family finances. Includes business news, stock and fund quotes, bulletin boards and chat rooms, and various financial planning calculators. You can create your own online portfolio to track your investments. Of particular interest: "Ask Cash Flo" lets you ask questions to a financial expert.

ArmChair Millionaire (www.armchairmillionaire.com). Designed for novice women investors. Offers a Get-Rich-Slowly-But-Surely Plan in Five Steps.

Beatrice's Web Guide (www.bguide.com). Provides a shortcut to some of the most useful sites on the Internet. Creates its own content, designed specifically for women. Includes sections on money, careers, home improvement, and much more.

StorkSite (www.storksite.com/index.html). Designed as a pregnancy and new parenting community on the Web. Includes areas where you can swap stories, find resources, and read various financial and general tips on how a new baby will affect your life.

The Buck Starts Here (www.talks.com/buck.html). Nancy Dunnan, a.k.a. "Auntie Spender," is a financial adviser whose articles appear weekly on the MoneyTalks Website. Though her articles cover a range of topics, she often addresses women's financial planning issues.

Advancing Women (www.advancingwomen.com). An international business and career network that focuses on strategy and employment for women. Features stories about women in business as well as a career center and a special section for Hispanic women. Can be viewed in English or Spanish.

BizWomen (www.bizwomen.com). An interactive site for successful women in business to network, exchange ideas, and provide support for each other.

Voices of Women (www.voicesofwomen.com). Features articles, a calendar of events, links, and a directory of women-friendly businesses. Of particular interest: the marketplace, a journal, and a resource guide.

WorkingWoman (workingwoman.com). A directory of women-owned businesses, professional services, and community services for WOWFactor (www.wowfactor.com). Contains a job search as well as contacts and commerce sections for networking and doing business.

Work At Home Moms (www.wahm.com). Editorials, links, classifieds, and business opportunities for women who work from home.

National Association for Female Executives (www.nafe.com). The latest news, job and information resources, and useful business tips.

Books

The 10 Minute Guide to Retirement for Women by Kerry Hannon (Macmillan General Reference, 1996). Discusses issues that affect a woman's retirement, such as smaller pensions, lower Social Security benefits, and a longer lifespan. This guide is filled with worksheets, tips on investments, and strategies to build wealth for women of all ages.

When Baby Boom Women Retire by Nancy Dailey (Praeger Pub Text, 1998. According to this author, fewer than 20% of Baby Boom women will experience a secure retirement. Marriage, education, occupation, and home ownership predict their future.

Women in Mid-Life: Planning for Tomorrow by Christopher Hayes (Harrington Park Press, 1992). Covers a host of pre- and postretirement planning issues for women. Includes a list of retirement planning resources.

Savvy Investing for Women: Strategies from a Self-Made Wall Street Millionaire by Marlene Jupiter (Prentice Hall, 1998). Jupiter provides a step-by-step guide for women investors.

Fair Share Divorce for Women by Kathleen Miller (Miller, 1995). Miller, a financial planner, offers case histories, charts, budgets, sample financial plans, settlement agreements, and vocational reports to illustrate the economic issues that must be addressed when ending a marriage. Also covered: long-term needs like pensions and retirement planning.

ABOUT THE AUTHORS

This is not just another "woman's book." We, the authors, are women ourselves, of course. But we're also financial planning professionals. Collectively, we have over 100 years of practical experience working with the financial problems facing young women and older women, single women and married women, widows and divorcees, and entrepreneurs and retirees at all levels of income, in varied situations.

The six of us came to Ernst & Young at different points in our careers. Some of us knew early on that we were meant to be planners, while some of us happened upon this profession by chance. In the pages that follow, you'll read about the particulars that led us here, why we're committed to excellence in our profession, and something about our philosophy in handling personal finances.

"I never heard anyone say, 'I started saving for retirement too early.'"

Elda Di Re is a partner in the personal financial counseling practice of Ernst & Young's New York office, specializing in financial planning and investment planning for wealthy family groups; estate planning; and estate, trust, and personal income tax services for executives and employees of major private and public companies. A graduate of the school of business at State University of New York at Albany, she holds a CPA as well as a CFP designation and is a frequent commentator representing Ernst & Young on national broadcast news and for the print media. She is a member of the American Institute of Certified Public Accountants and the New York State Society of Public Accountants. Elda is also an expert on the single life. She was recently married for the first time at age 36.

> After I had begun my career as a financial planner, I noticed that even though my friends were working at good jobs, they were not making enough money to support their lifestyles. Instead, they were using their credit lines to make purchases that were beyond their means—and falling deep into debt. None of my friends were bothered by this behavior. Typically, their response to my concern was: 'There'll be plenty of time to start saving and getting my finances in order after I get married. I'll worry about it then.'

That kind of thinking is a carryover from the past when a woman's future was determined almost exclusively by her husband's financial situation. It doesn't hold true in today's world. In fact, the opposite may almost be true. Because of the high divorce rate, a woman's natural longevity, and the fact that women are marrying later in life, it's likely that a woman will be living alone at some point in her life. Therefore, she needs to be financially self-sufficient—whether she plans to marry or not.

In most cases, I have to introduce women to the financial planning process. Once they start to understand the basics, however, I usually find that women, especially married women, are less fearful. They now know how to get along by themselves should something happen to their husbands. And sharing the burden of the family's financial responsibilities frees the couple from unnecessary pressures and fosters mutual cooperation and respect."

"If you can't support yourself, you can't make decisions about what to do with your life."

Andrea S. Markezin is a partner in the personal financial counseling practice in New York, specializing in the financial needs of family groups, integrating accounting and record-keeping, taxes, and investment needs. She has contributed to *Ernst & Young's Personal Financial Planning Guide* and other publications. She is a member of the Association of Certified Public Accountants and the New York State Society of Certified Public Accountants (NYSSCPA) and a former chair of the NYSSCPA's Committee for the Advancement of Women.

I always loved math. But my success with numbers, if you will, sort of happened by accident. In high school, I wasn't coordinated enough to make it as a cheerleader. I joined the math team instead. In college, I wavered between studying art and becoming an art historian or going for a financial degree. I realized I'd need a Ph.D. to pursue such a career in art history, and that jobs in that field were hard to come by. I majored in accounting instead.

After college, I went straight into public accounting. My plan was to get my CPA as quickly as possible, and then figure out what I wanted to do with the rest of my life. I never dreamed that I would stay in the accounting profession—or that I would like it. But I did. (Still do, in fact.) Initially, I worked on the audit staff and then the tax department for both corporate and individual clients. Today, however, I work exclusively with individuals and their family-owned businesses. It's a great fit for me. I like helping people work through their financial issues and reach their goals.

When I first started working as an accountant, there were few women in the field. Clients—especially male clients—weren't completely comfortable with me working on their accounts. But those days are long gone. Today, my approach is to make them feel comfortable so that they can easily discuss the financial and personal details of their lives. And since so much of financial planning revolves around a client's unique perspective of money—emotional, psychological, and otherwise—the ability to be part of a team with a client makes planning move smoothly. On the most basic level, I think that clients simply like to deal with qualified professionals who can relate to their life experiences.

I've been very lucky in my life's choices, thus far. My mother encouraged me (and my three siblings) to be self-sufficient and to believe that we could become whatever we wanted to be. I never thought for a minute that I couldn't pursue a certain career because I was a woman. My mother made different choices. In 1954, college didn't seem as important when everyone she knew was getting married and having children. She told me again and again, however, that I must be able to support myself, and that I shouldn't rely on my husband for financial support. How forward-thinking of her!

These days I try to pass that message on to my female clients. Even if your husband handles the bill-paying every month, you should understand your family's financial situation. How much money do you and your spouse earn combined? How much debt do you have? What about savings accounts and other investments? Every woman needs to know the answers to these questions so that she can make an intelligent financial decision for herself—by herself— if she has to.

"If you don't plan where you are going, you won't know when you get there."

Sylvia Pozarnsky is the partner in charge of the Personal Financial Counseling Group in Ernst & Young's Lake Michigan Region, headquartered in Chicago. During her 21-year career in financial planning, she has presented workshops and provided individual advice to thousands of women and men in different stages of their lives, with different amounts of knowledge about finances, and with different levels of income and net worth. The professionals in Sylvia's group currently provide workshops and individual counseling to over 100,000 individuals.

Sylvia holds a Bachelor of Music degree from the University of Iowa; a Master's Degree in Social Science from the University of Chicago; and a Master's of Business Administration in Finance from New York University. Sylvia is on the editorial board for *The Ernst & Young Tax Guide* and often appears on radio and television to discuss financial topics. She also serves on the Advisory Board for Ernst & Young Investment Advisers LLP.

Outside of Ernst & Young, Sylvia has continued her involvement with music by serving on the board of the Suzuki-Orff School for Young Musicians, an inner-city music school that brings together families of all economic and cultural backgrounds to learn about and expose their children to music.

Several years ago, at the seminars I frequently conducted across the country, I would recommend that the audience assess their finances every year. That means, compare your assets and liabilities to last year; list your income and expenses; and determine a savings goal for the coming year. That always sounded like a good plan. But at one of the meetings someone in the audience asked: "Do you follow your own advice?" I did not want to admit that I did not, so ever since then I have followed my own advice. Every January, I carefully review my own financial situation. I check to see if I've met my annual savings goals, and I compare this year's net worth to last year's. Then I draw up a list of financial resolutions for the new year—along with strategies to achieve them.

I grew up in a small town in South Dakota. My mother stayed home with us children, but both she and my father emphasized to my sister and me how important it was for *us* to be financially independent, not just our brothers.

I never planned to become a financial planner. The career didn't exist, per se, when I graduated from college in 1974. I was actually a music major in college, but couldn't find a career that was right for me. When my husband and I decided to move from Chicago to New York, however, I landed a job in E.F. Hutton's Personal Financial Planning Division.

I really enjoyed financial planning and decided to get an MBA. When I first began working in the field, women simply did not hold positions of power on Wall Street. Often, the thinking was that clients (read that as *male* clients) wouldn't want to work with women financial planners. But nothing could be further from the truth in today's market. Many clients—be they men or women—are more comfortable with women because of our approach to working with people. And we can generally empathize quite easily with our female clients.

Because I hold degrees in three vastly different subjects—music, social science, and finance—and because I've lived in both small towns and large cities, I'm confident that I can relate to just about anyone. Whenever I meet new people, I know I'll find a common interest and can easily discuss topics and issues that interest them. They in turn feel comfortable sharing their personal information and goals with me, which allows me to better help them meet their financial goals.

"It is vitally important that both spouses be fully involved in the family's financial planning."

Barbara J. Raasch is the partner in charge of investment advisory services and executive financial counseling at Ernst & Young's New York office. Barbara is a Chartered Financial Analyst (CFA), a Certified Public Accountant (CPA), a Certified Financial Planner (CFP) designee, and a Personal Financial Specialist (PFS). She is a member of the editorial board of *The Ernst & Young Tax Guide,* coauthor of the *Ernst & Young's Financial Planning Guide,* and an editor of *Ernst & Young's Financial Planning Reporter,* a bimonthly personal financial planning newsletter. She also writes a personal finance column for the *Milwaukee Journal* and the *Dallas Times Herald* that focuses on women's issues.

Barbara has held several leadership positions with Ernst & Young; she was the firm's first national director of investment counseling. Barbara is frequently quoted in financial periodicals such as *The Wall Street Journal,* and she appears regularly on national television. Barbara has been a guest on the Today Show, CNN, and Headline News.

My situation is somewhat unique. I got married when I was 21 years old. When my husband and I decided 3 years later to have children, we also decided that we wanted one of us to stay home. So we sat down together to discuss our career plans and our earning potential—and we determined that my husband would take on the primary caregiver role.

Over the years, however, my husband and I always managed our finances together, even though finance is my profession and he is Mr. Mom. That's allowed us to remain on equal footing. In many marriages, though, that isn't the case, especially in families where one person works and the other spouse stays at home to tend to the kids. Often, the breadwinning spouse starts to feel that the money is all his or hers, even though the stay-at-home spouse works too (although not for a paycheck).

With some clients, even though I suggest that both husband and wife participate in the financial planning, the stay-at-home spouse doesn't want to get involved. It's not that person's role. My feeling is that both spouses, whether they work for pay or not, make essential contributions to the well-being and security of the family. Therefore, they should both be involved in *all* financial planning decisions.

I've seen many wives who don't even know how much their husbands are making. That's terrible. If you view marriage as a partnership, then you ought to share the financial aspect of the union as well. Being left in the dark about your family's monetary situation creates a lot of stress for the nonworking spouse. You worry about what will happen if your spouse dies or if you get divorced, and if you can afford to retire comfortably and send the kids to a good college.

As a financial planner, I help many couples work through these very issues. It was this desire to help people better manage their cash flow and their investments, in fact, that drew me to the financial planning profession in the first place. I had been working as a tax accountant when I realized that several of my clients were able to retire comfortably. Other clients, however, were not. They were extremely anxious, I remember, about their ability to provide for their golden years.

I started taking a close look at the situations of the clients who were comfortably retired. I talked with them about their lives. And do you know what I discovered? It wasn't that they made more money, or never went on vacation, or worked a lot of overtime. Rather, they simply handled their money wisely. I quickly learned that all it takes to achieve your financial goals is a plan, the discipline to save early and consistently, and smart investments. And so I thought if I could help people manage their money better, I could make a tremendous difference in their lives. That's how I got started, and why I did.

"All things in moderation, particularly when it comes to the decisions involving your financial future."

Freida Kavouras is a senior manager in the personal financial counseling group in Ernst & Young's Lake Michigan Area, headquartered in Chicago. She specializes in employee group education services and has over 13 years of experience in providing communications and financial planning services to all levels of employees in the United States and abroad. She has delivered more than 500 financial education workshops to over 10,000 employees in the last 5 years. As the media representative for financial planning in Ernst & Young's Chicago office, Freida often appears on radio and television to discuss financial topics.

Freida is a Certified Public Accountant (CPA) as well as a Personal Financial Specialist (PFS). She is a member of the Personal Financial Planning Division of the American Institute of Certified Public Accountants and the Illinois Society of Certified Public Accountants. She holds a Bachelor of Science degree in accounting from The Pennsylvania State University.

I have three brothers. Yet I was always the most eager to help my father with financial matters related to his business and our family. Today, I'm the person my parents call if they have a financial question. I don't know that I ever actually planned to become a financial planner, but I suppose that's how it all started. Getting involved in my family's financial matters led me to major in accounting. After college, I decided to work in public accounting because I wanted to get experience with a variety of client situations.

Early in my career, I provided individual tax planning services to my clients and prepared hundreds of tax returns. I really enjoyed the personal aspect of working one on one with my clients. I helped them evaluate the tax consequences of their financial decisions, which led to providing estate planning and investment planning services to many of my executive clients. The move into financial planning seemed like a natural progression.

After 7 years of providing financial planning services for corporate executives and widows, I decided I wanted to focus on the educational aspects of financial planning and teach people to be more comfortable with their financial situation. So now I specialize in designing and delivering a variety of financial education workshop programs for corporate employees.

It's so gratifying to hear workshop participants tell me that they finally understand what investment changes they need to make or to learn that they're on track and following a wise strategy. The key to feeling confident about your finances is to make sure you understand and take the appropriate steps to realize your goals. Whether that means you should attend a course, read a financial journal, or work with an adviser depends on your own needs and situation.

"Impulse buying causes more money problems for my clients than any-thing else."

Paula Boyer Kennedy is the national director of *Ernst & Young's Financial Counseling HelpLine.* She is a Certified Public Accountant (CPA), a Personal Financial Specialist (PFS), and a Certified Financial Planner (CFP) designee. Paula received her Bachelor's Degree in English from Cornell University and her MBA in Finance and Accounting from Cornell's Johnson Graduate School of Management.

Paula's clients are employers, affinity groups, and financial institutions who want to offer financial counseling to large numbers of people. Ernst & Young's HelpLine, which Paula oversees, provides these groups with telephone counseling, financial planning analyses based on Ernst & Young's software, and administrative support.

Paula is past chairman and president of the Central New Jersey Society of the Institute of Certified Financial Planners. She has served on the Institute of Certified Financial Planners' National Technology Committee. She has also served on boards for the Amateur Computer Group of New Jersey, the Trenton Computer Festival, and the Baldwin School.

When my mother died in 1986, her estate was so mishandled that it is still not settled 12 years later. I was not an executor, so it was some time before I found out how bad the situation was. Once I did, I resolved to learn as much as I could about financial planning so that I could understand how it happened and, if possible, keep it from happening to anyone else. I became a Certified Financial Planner designee.

I tell the story of my mother's estate all the time. I think it's inspired a lot of people to do some serious estate planning. I can't stress enough that, if you have assets you'd like to protect, you must speak with a professional who specializes in trusts and estates to make sure that the things you care about pass to the people you love when you die.

I also tell the story of my divorce. When I separated from my first husband, I was on my own for the first time in my life. So I tried to make saving a game. How little could I spend this month and still survive? At one point, I pared my expenses so low that I was spending just $15 per week on food. (And it's probably the healthiest diet I ever had: fresh fruit and vegetables, mostly.) I went a whole year without buying clothes—and not a single person noticed. I still read a lot, but I got all my books at the library. Within that first year after my divorce, I managed to save half my take-home pay. That boosted by self-confidence enormously. Try it, if only for a short time, I tell my clients now. You'll see.

"Understanding how to manage your money is truly liberating, giving you the chance to do the things that are of value to you."

Jacqueline Hornstein, who is director of personal financial counseling educational communications at the National Personal Financial Counseling practice in New York, develops educational and marketing materials to support the firm's personal financial counseling practice. Jackie has 15 years' experience in writing, editing, and designing a wide range of materials in various media in the areas of financial planning, financial public relations, and employee benefits. She also has 10 years' experience as an educator. Jackie holds a B.A. in English from Alfred University and an M.A. and a Ph.D. in British and American Literature from New York University.

INDEX

A Public Service of Ernst & Young's Financial Education Program

www.moneyopolis.org

El ERNST & YOUNG LLP

SPECIAL CONSUMER OFFERS!

FREE one-year subscription to Ernst & Young's
Understanding Personal Finances newsletter!

 Get a one dollar rebate on your purchase of each of the following tax and financial planning books:

For Year-Round Tax Planning:
$1.00 Rebate for *The Ernst & Young Tax Saver's Guide 1999*

For Preparing Federal Tax Returns:
$1.00 Rebate for *The Ernst & Young Tax Guide 1999*

For Financial Planning:
$1.00 Rebate for *Ernst & Young's Financial Planning for Women*

OFFICIAL REFUND CERTIFICATE

I have purchased the Ernst & Young books checked below and have enclosed
the purchase receipt with the books' prices circled. Please send me the appropriate refund.

❏ **Yes.** Please start my FREE one-year subscription to Ernst & Young's *Understanding Personal Finances* newsletter.

❏ (1 book) $1 Refund   ❏ (2 books) $2 Refund   ❏ (3 books) $3 Refund

Mail to: The E&Y Tax and Financial Planning Guides Rebate Offer '99, P.O. Box 8104, Grand Rapids, MN 55745.

Name (Please Print)

Address

City   State   Zip

Signature

Store Where Purchased